Kirk Munroe

**Forward March**

A Tale of the Spanish-American war

Kirk Munroe

**Forward March**

*A Tale of the Spanish-American war*

ISBN/EAN: 9783337110574

Printed in Europe, USA, Canada, Australia, Japan

Cover: Foto ©ninafisch / pixelio.de

More available books at **www.hansebooks.com**

# FORWARD MARCH

KIRK MUNROE

# BOSTON
# PUBLIC
# LIBRARY

THE ROUGH RIDERS FOUGHT WITHOUT SEEING THE ENEMY

# "FORWARD, MARCH"
## A Tale of the
## SPANISH-AMERICAN WAR

By

KIRK MUNROE

AUTHOR OF

"THE PAINTED DESERT" "RICK DALE"
THE "MATE SERIES" ETC.

ILLUSTRATED

NEW YORK AND LONDON
HARPER & BROTHERS PUBLISHERS

# The Kirk Munroe Books
Illustrated—Jackets Printed in Colors

### The Mate Series
CAMPMATES     DORYMATES
CANOEMATES     RAFTMATES

### The Pacific Coast Series
RICK DALE     THE COPPER PRINCESS
SNOWSHOES AND SLEDGES     FOR THE MIKADO
THE FUR SEAL'S TOOTH     FORWARD MARCH
THE PAINTED DESERT     THE BLUE DRAGON
UNDER THE GREAT BEAR

Copyright, 1899, by HARPER & BROTHERS.

C-Z

# CONTENTS

| CHAPTER | PAGE |
|---|---|
| I. A Bowl of Roses | 1 |
| II. War is Declared | 9 |
| III. Rollo the Terror | 17 |
| IV. The Rough Riders at San Antonio | 24 |
| V. Ridge Becomes a Trooper | 33 |
| VI. Off for the War | 42 |
| VII. The Story of Hobson and the *Merrimac* | 51 |
| VIII. Charged with a Secret Mission | 59 |
| IX. Herman Dodley Interposes Difficulties | 68 |
| X. On the Cuban Blockade | 76 |
| XI. A Lively Experience of Cuban Hospitality | 85 |
| XII. Denounced by a Friend | 93 |
| XIII. To be Shot at Sunrise | 102 |
| XIV. Refugees in the Mountains | 111 |
| XV. Dionysio Captures a Spaniard | 119 |
| XVI. Asleep While on Guard | 126 |
| XVII. In the Hands of Spanish Guerillas | 134 |
| XVIII. Death of Señorita | 143 |
| XIX. Calixto Garcia the Cuban | 151 |
| XX. The Two Admirals | 160 |
| XXI. A Spaniard's Loyalty | 169 |

## CONTENTS

| CHAPTER | PAGE |
|---|---|
| XXII. ROLLO IN CUBA | 178 |
| XXIII. THE "TERRORS" IN BATTLE | 187 |
| XXIV. FACING SAN JUAN HEIGHTS | 196 |
| XXV. RIDGE WINS HIS SWORD | 205 |
| XXVI. MUTINY ON A TRANSPORT | 214 |
| XXVII. DESTRUCTION OF THE SPANISH SHIPS | 222 |
| XXVIII. LAST SHOT OF THE CAMPAIGN | 231 |
| XXIX. TWO INVALID HEROES | 239 |
| XXX. ROLLO MAKES PROPOSITIONS | 246 |

# ILLUSTRATIONS

The Rough Riders Fought Without Seeing
    the Enemy . . . . . . . . . . . . *Frontispiece*
"Silas Pine Gazed About Him with the Air
    of One Who Is Dazed" . . . . . . . . *Facing p.* 34
"'Him Holguin Spaniard. Now You Shoot
    Him,' Said the Cuban" . . . . . . . "    122
Ridge Escorts a Cuban Family into Santiago "    242

# "FORWARD, MARCH!"

# "FORWARD, MARCH!"

## CHAPTER I

### A BOWL OF ROSES

In the morning-room of a large, old-fashioned country-house, situated a few miles outside the city of New Orleans, sat a young man arranging a bowl of roses. Beside him stood a pretty girl, in riding costume, whose face bore a trace of petulance.

"Do make haste, Cousin Ridge, and finish with those stupid flowers. You have wasted half an hour of this glorious morning over them already!" she exclaimed.

"Wasted?" rejoined Ridge Norris, inquiringly, and looking up with a smile. "I thought you were too fond of flowers to speak of time spent in showing them off to best advantage as 'wasted.'"

"Yes, of course I'm fond of them," answered Spence Cuthbert, who was from Kentucky on a Mardi Gras visit to Dulce Norris, her school-chum and cousin by several removes, "but not fond enough to break an engagement on account of them."

"An engagement?"

"Certainly. You promised to go riding with me this morning."

"And so I will in a minute, when I have finished with these roses."

"But I want you to come this instant."

"And leave a duty unperformed?" inquired Ridge, teasingly.

"Yes ; now."

"In a minute."

"No. I won't wait another second."

With this the girl flung herself from the room, wearing a very determined expression on her flushed face.

Ridge rose to follow her, and then resumed his occupation as a clatter of hoofs on the magnolia-bordered driveway announced the arrival of a horseman.

"She won't go now that she has a caller to entertain," he said to himself.

But in this he was mistaken ; for within a minute another clatter of hoofs, mingled with the sound of laughing voices, gave notice of a departure, and, glancing from an open window, Ridge saw Spence Cuthbert ride gayly past in company with a young man whose face seemed familiar, but whose name he could not recall.

As they swept by both looked up laughing, while the horseman lifted his hat in a bow that was almost too sweeping to be polite.

"What did you say Ridge was doing?" he asked, as they passed beyond earshot.

"Arranging a bowl of roses," answered Spence.

"Nice occupation for a man," sneered the other.

"And he preferred doing that to riding with you?"

"So it seems."

"Well, I am not wholly surprised, for, as I remember him, he was a soft-hearted, Miss Nancy sort of a boy, who was always coddling sick kittens, or something of the kind, and never would go hunting because he couldn't bear to kill things. He apparently hadn't a drop of sporting blood in him, and I recall having to thrash him on one occasion because he objected to my shooting a bird. I thought of course, though, that he had outgrown all such nonsense by this time."

"There is no nonsense about him!" flashed out Spence, warmly; and then, to her companion's amazement, the girl began a most spirited defence of her absent cousin, during which she denounced in such bitter terms the taking of innocent lives under the name of "sport" that the other was finally thankful to change the conversation to a more congenial topic.

In the mean time Dulce Norris had entered the morning-room to find out why Spence had gone to ride with Herman Dodley instead of with Ridge, as had been arranged.

"Was that Herman Dodley?" asked the latter, without answering his sister's question.

"Yes, of course, but why do you ask with such a tragic air?"

"Because," replied Ridge, "I have heard reports

concerning him which, if confirmed, should bar the doors of this house against him forever."

"What do you mean, Ridge Norris? I'm sure Mr. Dodley bears as good a reputation as the majority of young men one meets in society. Of course since he has got into politics his character has been assailed by the other party; but then no one ever believes what politicians say of one another."

"No matter now what I mean," rejoined the young man. "Perhaps I will tell you after I have spoken to father on the subject, which I mean to do at once."

Ridge Norris, on his way to the library, where he hoped to find his father, was somewhat of a disappointment to his family. Born of a mother in whose veins flowed French and Spanish blood, and who had taught him to speak both languages, and of a New England father, who had spent his entire business life in the far South, Ridge had been reared in an atmosphere of luxury. He had been educated in the North, sent on a grand tour around the world, and had finally been given a position, secured through his father's influence, in a Japanese-American banking house. From Yokohama he had been transferred to the New York office, where, on account of a slight misunderstanding with one of his superiors, he had thrown up his position to return to his home only a few days before this story opens.

Now his family did not know what to do with

him. He disliked business, and would not study for a profession. He was a dear, lovable fellow, honest and manly in all his instincts; but indolent, fastidious in his tastes, and apparently without ambition. He was devoted to music and flowers, extremely fond of horses, which he rode more than ordinarily well, and had a liking for good books. He had, furthermore, returned from his travels filled with pride for his native land, and declaring that the United States was the only country in the world worth fighting and dying for.

Taking the morning's mail from the hand of a servant who had just brought it, Ridge entered his father's presence.

"Here are your letters, sir," he said, "but before you read them I should like a few moments' conversation with you."

"Certainly, son. What is it?"

As Ridge told what he had heard concerning Herman Dodley, the elder man's brows darkened; and, when the recital was finished, he said:

"I fear all this is true, and have little doubt that Dodley is no better than he should be; but, unfortunately, I am so situated at present that I cannot forbid him the house. I will warn Dulce and her friend against him; but just now I am not in a position to offend him."

"Why, father!" cried Ridge, amazed to hear his usually fearless and self-assertive parent adopt this tone. "I thought that you were—"

"Independent of all men," interrupted the other.

finishing the sentence. "So I believed myself to be. But I am suddenly confronted by business embarrassments that force me temporarily to adopt a different policy. Truly, Ridge, we are threatened with such serious losses that I am making every possible sacrifice to try and stem the tide. I have even placed our summer home on the Long Island coast in an agent's hands, and am deeply grieved that you should have thrown up a position, promising at least self-support, upon such slight provocation."

"But he ordered me about as though I were a servant, instead of requesting me to do things in a gentlemanly way."

"And were you not a servant?"

"No, sir, I was not—at least, not in the sense of being amenable to brutal commands. I was not, nor will I ever be, anybody's slave."

"Oh well, my boy!" replied the elder, with a deep sigh, "I fear you will live to discover by sad experience that pride is the most expensive of earthly luxuries, and that one must consent to obey orders long before he can hope to issue commands. But we will discuss your affairs later, for now I must look over my letters."

While Mr. Norris was thus engaged, Ridge opened the morning paper, and glanced carelessly at its headlines. Suddenly he sprang to his feet with a shout, his dark face glowing and his eyes blazing with excitement.

"By heavens, father!" he cried, "the United States battle-ship *Maine* has been blown up in

Havana Harbor with a loss of two hundred and sixty of her crew. If that doesn't mean war, then nothing in the world's history ever did. You needn't worry about me any more, sir, for my duty is clearly outlined."

"What do you propose to do?" asked the elder man, curiously. "Will you try to blow up a Spanish battle-ship in revenge?"

"No, sir. But I shall enlist at the very first call to arms, and offer my life towards the thrashing of the cowards who have perpetrated this incredible crime."

Thrilled to the core by the momentous news he had just read, Ridge hastened to impart it to his mother and sister. At the same time he ordered a horse on which he might ride to the city for further details of the stupendous event. As he was about to depart, Spence Cuthbert and her escort, returning from their ride, dashed up to the doorway.

"Have you heard the news?" cried Ridge, barely nodding to Dodley.

"Yes," replied Spence. "Isn't it dreadful? Mr. Dodley told me all about it, and after hearing it I couldn't bear to ride any farther, so we came back."

"I wish he had told me before you started," said Ridge, "so that I might have been in the city long ago."

"You were so busily and pleasantly engaged with your roses that I hesitated to interrupt you," murmured Herman Dodley. "Now, however, if I can be of any assistance to you in the city, pray consider me at your service."

"Can you assist me, sir, to obtain a commission in the army that will be summoned to visit a terrible punishment upon Spain for her black treachery?"

"Undoubtedly I could, and of course I would do so with pleasure if the occasion should arise. But there won't be any war. The great Yankee nation is too busy accumulating dollars to fight over a thing of this kind. We will demand a money indemnity, it will be promptly paid, and the whole affair will quickly be forgotten."

"Sir!" cried Ridge, his face pale with passion. "The man who utters such words is at heart a traitor to his country."

"If it were not for the presence of ladies, I would call you to account for that remark," muttered Dodley. "As it is, I shall not forget it. Ladies, I have the honor to wish you a very good-morning."

With this the speaker, who had not dismounted, turned his horse's head and rode away.

## CHAPTER II

### WAR IS DECLARED

NEVER was the temper and patience of the American people more sorely tried than by the two months of waiting and suspense that followed the destruction of their splendid battle-ship. The *Maine* had entered Havana Harbor on a friendly visit, been assigned to a mooring, which was afterwards changed by the Spanish authorities, and three weeks later, without a suspicion of danger having been aroused or a note of warning sounded, she was destroyed as though by a thunder-bolt. It was nearly ten o'clock on the night of Tuesday, February 15th. Taps had sounded and the crew were asleep in their hammocks, when, by a terrific explosion, two hundred and fifty-eight men and two officers were hurled into eternity, sixty more were wounded, and the superb battle-ship was reduced to a mass of shapeless wreckage.

It was firmly believed throughout the United States that this appalling disaster was caused by a submarine mine, deliberately placed near the mooring buoy to which the *Maine* had been moved, to be exploded at a favorable opportunity by Spanish hands.

The Spaniards, on the other side, claimed and strenuously maintained that the only explosion was that of the ship's own magazines, declaring in support of this theory that discipline on all American men-of-war was so lax as to invite such a catastrophe at any moment.

To investigate, and settle if possible, this vital question, a Court of Inquiry, composed of four prominent naval officers, was appointed. They proceeded to Havana, took volumes of testimony, and, after six weeks of most searching investigation, made a report to the effect that the *Maine* was destroyed by two distinct explosions, the first of which was that of a mine located beneath her, and causing a second explosion — of her own magazines — by concussion.

During these six weeks the country was in a ferment. For three years war had raged in Cuba, where the natives were striving to throw off the intolerable burden of Spanish oppression and cruelty. In all that time the sympathies of America were with the struggling Cubans; and from every State of the Union demands for intervention in their behalf, even to the extent of going to war with Spain, had grown louder and more insistent, until it was evident that they must be heeded. With the destruction of the *Maine* affairs reached such a crisis that the people, through their representatives in Congress, demanded to have the Spanish flag swept forever from the Western hemisphere.

In vain did President McKinley strive for a

peaceful solution of the problem; but with both nations bent on war, he could not stem the tide of popular feeling. So, on the 20th of April he was obliged to demand from Spain that she should, before noon of the 23d, relinquish forever her authority over Cuba, at the same time withdrawing her land and naval forces from that island. The Spanish Cortes treated this proposition with contempt, and answered it by handing his passports to the American Minister at Madrid, thereby declaring war against the great American republic.

At this time Spain believed her navy to be more than a match for that of the United States, and that, with nearly two hundred thousand veteran, acclimated troops on the island of Cuba, she was in a position to resist successfully what she termed the "insolent demands of the Yankee pigs."

On this side of the Atlantic, Congress had appropriated fifty millions of dollars for national defence, the navy was being strengthened by the purchase of additional ships at home and abroad, fortifications were being erected along the entire coast, harbors were mined, and a powerful fleet of warships was gathered at Key West, the point of American territory lying nearest the island of Cuba.

Then came the President's call for 125,000 volunteers, followed a few weeks later by a second call for 75,000 more. This was the summons for which our young friend, Ridge Norris, had waited so impatiently ever since that February morning when he had arranged a bowl of roses and read the startling news of the *Maine's* destruction.

No one in all the country had been more impatient of the long delay than he; for it had seemed to him perfectly evident from the very first that war must be declared, and he was determined to take an active part in it at the earliest opportunity. His father was willing that he should go, his mother was bitterly opposed; Dulce begged him to give up his design, and even Spence Cuthbert's laughing face became grave whenever the subject was mentioned, but the young man was not to be moved from his resolve.

Mardi Gras came and passed, but Ridge, though escorting his sister and cousin to all the festivities, took only a slight interest in them. He was always slipping away to buy the latest papers or to read the bulletins from Washington.

"Would you go as a private, son?" asked his father one evening when the situation was being discussed in the family circle.

"No, no! If he goes at all—which Heaven forbid —it must be as an officer," interposed Mrs. Norris, who had overheard the question.

"Of course a gentleman would not think of going as anything else," remarked Dulce, conclusively.

"I believe there were gentlemen privates on both sides during the Civil War," said Spence Cuthbert, quietly.

"Of course," admitted Dulce, "but that was different. Then men fought for principles, but now they are going to fight for—for—"

"The love of it, perhaps," suggested the girl from Kentucky.

"You know I don't mean that," cried Dulce. "They are going to fight because—"

"Because their country calls them," interrupted Ridge, with energy, "and because every true American endorses Decatur's immortal toast of 'Our Country. May she always be in the right; but, right or wrong, our country.' Also because in the present instance we believe it is as much our right to save Cuba from further oppression at the hands of Spain as it always is for the strong to interpose in behalf of the weak and helpless. For these reasons, and because I do not seem fit for anything else, I am going into the city to-morrow to enlist in whatever regiment I find forming."

"Oh, my boy! my boy!" cried Mrs. Norris, flinging her arms around her son's neck, "do not go to-morrow. Wait a little longer, but one week, until we can see what will happen. After that I will not seek further to restrain you. It is your mother who prays."

"All right, mother dear, I will wait a few days to please you, though I cannot see what difference it will make."

So the young man waited as patiently as might be a week longer, and before it was ended the whole country was ringing with the wonderful news of Admiral George Dewey's swift descent upon the

Philippine Islands with the American Asiatic squadron. With exulting heart every American listened to the thrilling story of how this modern Farragut stood on the bridge of the *Olympia*, and, with a fine contempt for the Spanish mines known to be thickly planted in the channel, led his ships into Manila Bay. Almost before the startled Spaniards knew of his coming he had safely passed their outer line of defences, and was advancing upon their anchored fleet of iron-clad cruisers. An hour later he had completely destroyed it, silenced the shore batteries, and held the proud city of Manila at his mercy. All this he had done without the loss of a man or material damage to his ships, an exploit so incredible that at first the world refused to believe it.

To Ridge Norris, who had spent a week in the Philippines less than a year before, the whole affair was of intense interest, and he bitterly regretted not having remained in the Far East that he might have participated in that glorious fight.

"I would gladly have shipped as a sailor on the *Olympia* if I had only known what was in store for her!" he exclaimed; "but a chance like that, once thrown away, never seems to be offered again."

"But, my boy, it is better now," said Mrs. Norris, with a triumphant smile. "Then you would have been only a common seaman; one week ago you would have enlisted as a common soldier. Now you may go as an officer—what you will call a lieutenant—with the chance soon to become a captain, and perhaps a general. Who can tell?"

"Whatever do you mean, mother?"

"What I say, and it is even so; for have I not the promise of the Governor himself? But your father will tell you better, for he knows what has been done."

So Ridge went to his father, who confirmed what he had just heard, saying:

"Yes, son; your mother has exerted her influence in your behalf, and procured for you the promise of a second-lieutenant's commission, provided I am willing to pay for the honor."

"How, father?"

"By using my influence to send Herman Dodley to the Legislature as soon as he comes back from the war."

"Is Dodley going into the army?"

"Yes. He is to be a major."

"And would you help to send such a man to the Legislature?"

"If you wanted to be a lieutenant badly enough to have me do so, I would."

"Father, you know I wouldn't have you do such a thing even to make me President of the United States!"

"Yes, son, I know it."

And the two, gazing into each other's eyes, understood each other perfectly.

"I would rather go as a private, father."

"I would rather have you, son; though it would be a great disappointment to your mother."

"She need not know, for I will go to some distant camp before enlisting. I wouldn't serve in the same regiment with Herman Dodley, anyhow."

"Of course not, son."

"I suppose his appointment is political—as well as the one intended for me?"

"Yes; and so it is with every other officer in the regiment."

"That settles it. I would sooner join the Cubans than fight under the leadership of mere politicians. So, when I do enlist, it will be in some regiment where the word politics is unknown, even if I have to go into the regular army."

"Son, I am prouder of you than I ever was before. What will you want in the way of an outfit?"

"One hundred dollars, if you can spare so much."

"You shall have it, with my blessing."

So it happened that, a few days later, Ridge Norris started for the war, though without an idea of where he should find it or in what capacity he should serve his country.

## CHAPTER III

### ROLLO THE TERROR

On the evening when Ridge decided to take his departure for the seat of war he was driven into the city by his father, who set him down near the armory of the regiment in which he had been offered a lieutenant's commission—for a consideration.

"I don't want you to tell me where you are going, son," said Mr. Norris, "for I would rather be able to say, with a clear conscience, that I left you at headquarters, and beyond that know nothing of your movements."

"All right, father," replied the young fellow. "I won't tell you a thing about it, for I don't know where I am going any more than you do."

"Then good-bye, my boy, and may Almighty God restore you to us safe and well when the war is over. Here is the money you asked for, and I only wish I were able to give you ten times the sum. Be careful of it, and don't spend it recklessly, for you must remember that we are poor folk now."

Thus saying, the elder man slipped a roll of crisp bills into his son's hand, kissed him on the cheek, a thing he had not done before in a dozen years, and, without trusting his voice for another word, drove rapidly away.

For a minute Ridge stood in the shadow of the massive building, listening with a full heart to the rattle of departing wheels. Then he stooped to pick up the hand-bag, which was all the luggage he proposed to take with him. As he did so, two men brushed past him, and he overheard one of them say:

"Yes, old Norris was bought cheap. A second-lieutenancy for his cub fixed him. The berth'll soon be vacant again though, for the boy hasn't sand enough to—"

Here the voice of the speaker was lost as the two turned into the armory.

"Thanks for your opinion, Major Dodley," murmured Ridge; "that cheap berth will be vacant sooner than you think."

Then, picking up his "grip," the young fellow walked rapidly away towards the railway station. He was clad in a blue flannel shirt, brown canvas coat, trousers, and leggings, and wore a brown felt hat, the combination making up a costume almost identical with that decided upon as a Cuban campaign uniform for the United States army. Ridge had provided himself with it in order to save the carrying of useless luggage. In his "grip" he had an extra shirt, two changes of under-flannels, several pairs of socks, a pair of stout walking-shoes, and a few toilet articles, all of which could easily be stowed in an army haversack.

Our hero's vaguely formed plan, as he neared the station, was to take the first east-bound train and make his way to one of the great camps of mobilization, either at Chickamauga, Georgia, or Tampa, Florida, where he hoped to find some regiment in which he could conscientiously enlist. A train from the North had just reached the station as he entered it; but, to his disgust, he found that several hours must elapse before one would be ready to bear him eastward.

He was too excited to wait patiently, but wandered restlessly up and down the long platform. All at once there came to his ears the sound of a familiar voice, and, turning, he saw, advancing towards him, in the full glare of an electric light, three men, all young and evidently in high spirits. One, thin, brown, and wiry, was dressed as a cowboy of the Western plains. Another, who was a giant in stature, wore a golf suit of gray tweed; while the third, of boyish aspect, whom Ridge recognized as the son of a well-known New York millionaire, was clad in brown canvas much after his own style, though he also wore a prodigious revolver and a belt full of cartridges.

He was Roland Van Kyp, called "Rollo" for short, one of the most persistent and luxurious of globe-trotters, who generally travelled in his own magnificent steam-yacht *Royal Flush*, on board of which he had entertained princes and the cream of foreign nobility without number. Everybody knew Van Kyp, and everybody liked him; he was such a genial soul, ever ready to bother himself over some other fellow's trouble, but never intimating that he had any of his own; reckless, generous, happy-go-lucky, always getting into scrapes and out of them with equal facility. To his more intimate friends he had been variously known as " Rollo Abroad," " Rollo in Love," " Rollo in Search of a Wife," or " Rollo at Play," and when Ridge became acquainted with him in Yokohama he was " Rollo in Japan."

He now recognized our hero at a glance, and sprang forward with outstretched hand.

" Hello, Norris, my dear boy!" he cried. "Whatever brings you here? Thought you were still far away in the misty Orient, doing the grand among the little brown Japs, while here you are in flannel and canvas as though you were a major-general in the regular army. What does it mean? Are you one of us? Have you too become a man of war, a fire-eater, a target for Mausers? Have you enlisted under the banner of the screaming eagle?"

" Not yet," laughed Ridge, " but I am on my way East to do so in the first regiment uncontaminated by politics that I can find."

" Then, old man, you don't want to go East. You want to come West with us. There is but one regiment such as you have named, and it is mine; for, behold! I am now Rollo in the Army, Rollo the Rough Rider, Rollo the Terror. Perhaps it would be more becoming, though, to say 'Ours,' for we are all in it."

" I should rather imagine that it would," growled

he of the golf stockings, now joining in the conversation. "And, 'Rollo in Disguise,' suppose you present us to your friend; for, if I am not mistaken, he is a gentleman of whom I have heard and would like much to meet."

"Of course you would," responded Rollo, " and I beg your pardon for not having introduced you at once; but in times of war, you know, one is apt to neglect the amenities of a more peaceful existence. Mr. Norris, allow me to present my friend and pupil in the art of football-playing—"

" Oh, come off," laughed the big man.

" Pupil, as I was saying when rudely interrupted," continued Rollo, " Mr. Mark Gridley."

" Not Gridley, the famous quarter-back!" exclaimed Ridge, holding out his hand.

" That's him," replied Van Kyp.

" And aren't you Norris, the gentleman rider?" asked Gridley.

" I have ridden," acknowledged Ridge.

" So has this my other friend and fellow-soldier," cried Van Kyp. " Norris, I want you to know Mr. Silas Pine, of Medora, North Dakota, a bad man from the Bad Lands, a bronco-buster by profession, who has also consented to become a terror to Spaniards in my company."

" Have you a company, then?" asked Ridge, after he had acknowledged this introduction.

"I have—that is, I belong to one; but, in the sense you mean, you must not use the word company. That is a term common to 'doughboys,' who, as you doubtless know, are merely uniformed pedestrians; but we of the cavalry always speak of our immediate fighting coterie as a 'troop.' Likewise the 'battalion' of the inconsequent doughboy has for our behoof been supplanted by the more formidable word 'squadron,' to show that we are *de jure* as well as *de facto* men of war. Sabe?"

"Then you are really in the cavalry?" asked Ridge, while laughing at this nonsense.

"Yes, I really am, or rather I really shall be when I get there; for though enlisted and sworn in, we haven't yet joined or been sworn at."

"What is your regiment?"

"You mean our 'command.' Why, didn't I tell you? 'Teddy's Terrors,' Roosevelt's Rough Riders. First Volunteer Cavalry, U.S.A., Colonel Leonard Wood commanding."

"The very one!" cried Ridge. "Why didn't I think of it before? How I wish I could join it."

"And why not?"

"I thought there were so many applications that the ranks were more than full."

"So there may be, but, like lots of other full things, there's always room for one more, if he's of the right sort."

"Do you imagine I would stand the slightest chance of getting in?"

"I should say you would. With me ready to use my influence in your behalf, and me and Teddy the chums we are, besides you being the rider you are. Why the first question Teddy asks of an applicant is, 'Can you ride a horse?' And when you answer, 'Sir, I am the man who wrote—I mean who won the silver hurdles at the last Yokohama gym.', he'll be so anxious to have you in the regiment that he'd resign in your favor rather than lose you. Oh, if I only had your backing do you suppose I'd be a mere private Terror? No, siree, I'd be corporal or colonel or something of that kind, sure as you're born. But come on, let's get aboard, for there's the tinkle-bell a-tinkling."

"I haven't bought my ticket yet," remonstrated Ridge.

"You won't need one, son. We're travelling in my private car 'Terror'—used to be named 'Buster,' you know—and the lay-out is free to all my friends."

Thus it happened that kindly Fate had interposed to guide our hero's footsteps, but it was not until he found himself seated in the luxurious smoking-room of Rollo Van Kyp's private railway carriage that it occurred to him to inquire whither they were bound.

"To the plains of Texas, my boy, and the city of San Antonio de Bexar, where Teddy and his Terrors are impatiently awaiting our advent," replied Rollo. At the same time he touched an electric bell and ordered a supper, which, when it appeared, proved to be one of the daintiest meals that Ridge Norris had ever eaten.

## CHAPTER IV

### THE ROUGH RIDERS AT SAN ANTONIO

DURING the remainder of that night and all the following day the train to which the "Terror" was attached sped westward through the rich lowlands of southern Louisiana and across the prairies of Texas. It crossed the tawny flood of the Mississippi on a huge railway ferry to Algiers, and at New Iberia it passed a side-tracked train filled with State troops bound for Baton Rouge. Early the next morning at Houston, Texas, it drew up beside another train-load of soldiers on their way to Austin. To the excited mind of our young would-be cavalryman it seemed as though the whole country was under arms and hurrying towards the scene of conflict. Was he not going in the wrong direction, after all? And would not those other fellows get to Cuba ahead of him in such force that there would be no Spaniards left for the Riders to fight? This feeling was so increased upon reaching the end of the journey, where he saw two San Antonio companies starting for the East, that he gave expression to his fears, whereupon Van Kip responded, promptly:

"Don't you fret, old man. We'll get there in plenty of time. Teddy's gone into this thing for blood, and he's got the inside track on information, too. Fixed up a private ticker all of his own before he left Washington, and when he gets ready to start he'll go straight to the front without a sidetrack. Oh, I know him and his ways! for, as I've said before, we're great chums, me and Teddy. I shouldn't wonder if he'd be at the station to meet us."

To Rollo's disappointment, neither Lieutenant-Colonel Roosevelt nor any one else was on hand to welcome the Riders' new recruits, but this was philosophically explained by the young New-Yorker on the ground that he had thoughtlessly neglected to telegraph their coming. Being thus left to their own devices, and anxious to join their regiment as quickly as possible, the three who were already enlisted engaged a carriage to convey them to the fair-grounds, just beyond the city limits, where the Riders were encamped, leaving Ridge to occupy the car in solitary state until morning.

"You just stay here and make yourself cozy," said Rollo, "while we go and get our bearings. I'll see Teddy and fix things all right for you, so that you can come out and join us bright and early tomorrow. So long. Robert, take good care of Mr. Norris, and see that he has everything to make him comfortable."

This order was delivered to the colored steward of the car, and in another minute the excited trio had rattled away, leaving Ridge to a night of luxurious loneliness.

To occupy his time he took a brisk walk into the city, and reached the Alamo Plaza before he knew where he was. Then, suddenly, he realized; for, half-hidden by a great ugly wooden building, used as a grocery-store, he discovered an antiquated, half-ruinous little structure of stone and stucco that he instantly recognized, from having seen it pictured over and over again. It was the world-renowned Alamo, one of the most famous monuments to liberty in America; and, hastening across the plaza, Ridge stood reverently before it, thrilled with the memory of Crockett and Bowie, Travis and Bonham, who, more than half a century before, together with their immediate band of heroes, here yielded up their lives that Texas might be free.

Ridge was well read in the history of the Lone Star State, and now he strove to picture to himself the glorious tragedy upon which those grim walls had looked. As he thus stood, oblivious to his surroundings, he was recalled to them by a voice close at hand, saying, as though in soliloquy:

" What a shame that so sacred a monument should be degraded by the vulgarity of its environment!"

"Is it not?" replied Ridge, turning towards the speaker. The latter was a squarely built man, about forty years of age, with a face expressive of intense determination, which at the moment was partially hidden by a slouch hat pulled down over the forehead, and a pair of spectacles. He was clad in brown canvas, very much as was Ridge himself; but except for facings of blue on collar and sleeve he wore no distinctive mark of rank. For a few minutes the two talked of the Alamo and all that it represented. Then the stranger asked, abruptly,

"Do you belong to the Rough Riders?"

"No," replied Ridge, "but I hope to. I am going to make application to join them to-morrow, or rather I believe a friend is making it for me this evening. Are you one of them, sir?"

"Yes, though I have not yet joined. In fact, I have only just reached San Antonio."

"So have I," said Ridge. "I came in on the Eastern train less than an hour ago."

"Strange that I did not see you," remarked the other. "Were you in the Pullman?"

"No, I was in a private car."

"I noticed that there was one, though I did not know to whom it belonged. Is it yours?"

"Oh no!" laughed Ridge. "I am far too poor to own anything so luxurious. It belongs to my friend, Mr. Roland Van Kyp, of New York."

"Sometimes called Rollo?"

"Yes; do you know him?"

"I have met him. Is he the one who is to use his influence in your behalf?"

"Yes."

"Can you ride a horse?"

"I have ridden," rejoined Ridge, modestly.

"Where?"

"In many places. The last was Japan, where I

won the silver hurdles of the Yokohama gymkana."

"Indeed! And your name is—"

"Ridge Norris," replied the young man.

"I have heard the name, and am glad to know you, Mr. Norris. Now I must bid you good-evening. Hope we shall meet again, and trust you may be successful in joining our regiment."

With this the stranger walked rapidly away, leaving Ridge somewhat puzzled by his manner, and wishing he had asked his name.

About eight o'clock the next morning, as Ridge, waited on by the attentive Robert, was sitting down to the daintily appointed breakfast-table of Rollo Van Kyp's car, the young owner himself burst into the room.

"Hello, Norris!" he cried. "Just going to have lunch? Don't care if I join you. Had breakfast hours ago, you know, and a prime one it was. Scouse, slumgullion, hushpuppy, dope without milk, and all sorts of things. I tell you life in camp is fine, and no mistake. Slept in a dog-tent last night with a full-blooded Indian—Choctaw or something of that kind, one of the best fellows I ever met. Couldn't catch on to his name, but it doesn't make any difference, for all the boys call him 'Hully Gee' —'Hully' for short, you know.

"But such fun and such a rum crowd you never saw! Why, there are cowboys, ranchers, prospectors, coppers, ex-sheriffs, sailors, mine-owners, men from every college in the country, tennis champions, football-players, rowing-men, polo-players, planters, African explorers, big-game hunters, ex-revenue-officers, and Indian-fighters, besides any number of others who have led the wildest kinds of life, all chock-full of stories, and ready to fire 'em off at a touch of the trigger. Teddy hasn't come yet, and so I haven't been able to do anything for you; but you must trot right out, all the same, and join our mess. Besides, I want you to pick out a horse for me, something nice and quiet, 'cause I'm not a dead game rider, you know. Same time he must be good to look at, sound, and fit in every respect. I've already bought one this morning, a devilish pretty little mare, on Sile Pine's say-so that she was gentle, but after a slight though very trying experience, I'm afraid a bronco-buster's ideas of gentleness and mine don't exactly agree."

"Why? Did she throw you?" asked Ridge.

"Well, she didn't exactly throw me. I was merely projected about a thousand yards as though from a dynamite-gun, and then the brute tried to chew me up. You see she's a Mexican—what Mark Twain would call a 'genuine Mexican plug'—and doesn't seem to sabe United States; for when I began to reason with her she simply went wild. I left her tearing through the camp like a steam-cyclone, and if we find anything at all to show where it was located, it is more than I hope for. But there's a new lot of prime-looking cattle just arrived, and they are going like hot cakes; so come along quick and help me get something rideable."

Half an hour later Ridge found himself in the first army camp he had ever visited, amid a body of men the most heterogeneous but typically American ever gathered together. Millionaire dudes and clubmen from the great Eastern cities fraternized with the wildest representatives of far Western life. Men of every calling and social position, all wearing blue flannel shirts and slouch hats, were here mingled on terms of perfect equality. They were drilling, shooting, skylarking, playing cards, performing incredible feats on horseback, cooking, eating, singing, yelling, and behaving in every respect like a lot of irrepressible schoolboys out for a holiday. Here a red-headed Irish corporal damned the awkwardness of a young Boston swell, fresh from Harvard, who had been detailed as cook in a company kitchen ; while, close at hand, a New-Yorker of the bluest blood was washing dishes with the deftness gained from long experience on a New Mexican sheep-ranch.

As Ridge and Rollo passed through one of the canvas-bordered streets of this unique camp, the former suddenly leaped aside with an exclamation of alarm. An unknown beast, fortunately chained, had made a spring at him, with sharp claws barely missing his leg.

"You mustn't mind a little thing like that," laughed Rollo, with the air of one to whom such incidents were of every-day occurrence. "It's only 'Josephine,' a young mountain lion from Arizona, and our regimental mascot. She's very playful."

"So it seems," replied Ridge, "and I suppose I shall learn to like her if I join the regiment; but the introduction was a little startling."

A short distance beyond the camp was gathered a confused group of officers, troopers, men in citizen's dress, some of whom were swart-faced Mexicans, and horses. To this Rollo led the way; and, as the new-comers drew near they saw that for a moment all eyes were directed towards a man engaged in a fierce struggle with a horse. The animal was a beautiful chestnut mare with slender limbs, glossy coat, and superb form. Good as she was to look upon, she was just then exhibiting the spirit of a wild-cat or anything else that is most savage and untamable, and was attempting, with desperate struggles, to throw and kill the man who rode her. He was our recent acquaintance, Silas Pine, bronco-buster from the Bad Lands, who, with clinched teeth and rigid features, was in full practice of his chosen profession.

All at once, no one could tell how, but with a furious effort the mare shook off her hated burden, and, with a snort of triumph, dashed madly away. The man was flung heavily to the ground, where he lay motionless.

"That's my horse," remarked Rollo, quietly, "and Sile undertook to either break or kill her. Nice, gentle beast, isn't she? Hello, you're in luck, for there's Roosevelt now. Oh, Teddy! I say, Teddy!"

Two officers on horseback were approaching the scene, and in one of them Ridge recognized his chance acquaintance of the evening before. Towards this individual Van Kyp was running.

All at once the second officer, who proved to be Colonel Leonard Wood of the regular army, now commanding the Riders, turned to a sergeant who stood near by, and said, sharply :

"Arrest that man and take him to the guardhouse. We have had enough of this 'Teddy' business, and I want it distinctly understood that hereafter Lieutenant-Colonel Roosevelt is to receive the title of his rank from every man in this command."

In another moment Rollo Van Kyp had been seized by the brawny sergeant, lately a mounted policeman of New York city, and was being marched protestingly away, leaving Ridge bewildered, friendless, and uncertain what to do.

## CHAPTER V

### RIDGE BECOMES A TROOPER

WHILE our hero stood irresolute, he saw Silas Pine gain a sitting posture, and gaze about him with the air of one who is dazed.

"Are you badly hurt?" inquired Ridge, as he reached the man's side.

"I don't know," replied Silas, moving his limbs cautiously, and feeling of various portions of his body to ascertain if any bones were broken. "Reckon not. But will you kindly tell me what happened?"

"You were breaking in Mr. Van Kyp's horse, and got thrown," replied Ridge, as gravely as possible, but with an irrepressible smile lurking in the corners of his mouth.

The bronco-buster, noting this, became instantly filled with wrath.

"Got thrown, did I? And you think it a thing to laugh at, do you? Well, you wouldn't if you'd been in my place. I claim to know something about hosses, and I tell you that's not one at all. She's a 'hoss devil,' that's what she is, for all she looks quiet as a sheep. But I'll kill her yet or die trying to tame her; for such a brute's not fit to live."

"Won't you let me try my hand at it first?" asked Ridge.

"You? you?" exclaimed the man in contemptuous amazement. "Yes, I will, for if you are fool enough to tackle her, you are only fit to be killed, and might as well die now as later. Oh yes, young feller, you can try it; only leave us a lock of your hair to remember you by, and we'll give you a first-class funeral."

By this time two Mexican riders, who had started in pursuit of the runaway animal, had cornered it in an angle of the high fence surrounding the camp-grounds, flung their ropes over its head, and were dragging it back, choking and gasping for breath, to the scene of its recent triumph.

"Hold on!" cried Ridge in Spanish, running towards them as he spoke, and shouting commands in their own language.

Slipping the cruel ropes from the neck of the quivering mare, that stared at him with wild eyes, Ridge petted and soothed her, at the same time talking gently in Spanish, a tongue that she showed signs of understanding by pricking forward her shapely ears. After a little Ridge led the animal to a watering-trough, where she drank greedily, and then into camp, where he begged a handful of sugar from one of the cooks.

Some ten minutes later, without having yet attempted to gain the saddle, he led the mare back

"SILAS PINE GAZED ABOUT HIM WITH THE AIR OF ONE IS DAZED"

to the place from which they had started, all the while talking to her and stroking her glossy neck.

"Why don't you ride?" growled Silas Pine, who still remained on the scene of his recent discomfiture, and had watched Ridge's movements curiously. "Any fool can lead a hoss to water and back again."

For answer Ridge gathered up the bridle reins, and placing his hands on pommel and cantle, sprang lightly into the saddle.

The mare laid her ears flat back and began to tremble with rage, but her rider, bending low over the proud neck, talked to her as though she were a human being, and in another moment they were off like the wind. Twice they circled the entire grounds at a speed as yet unequalled in the camp, and then drew up sharply where Silas Pine still stood awaiting them.

"Mr. Norris," said that individual, stepping forward, "I owe you an apology, and must say I never saw a finer—"

Just here the mare snapped viciously at the bronco-buster, from whose spurs her flanks were still bleeding, and leaped sideways with so sudden a movement that any but a most practiced rider would have been flung to the ground. Without appearing in the least disconcerted by this performance, Ridge began to reply to Silas Pine, but was interrupted by the approach of the two mounted officers, who had watched the recent lesson in bronco-breaking with deep interest.

"Can you do that with any horse?" inquired Lieutenant-Colonel Roosevelt, abruptly.

"I believe I can, sir," replied Ridge, lifting his hand in salute.

"I heard you talking in Spanish. Do you speak it fluently?"

"As well as I do English, sir."

"I believe you wish to enlist in this regiment?"

"I do, sir."

"You are a friend of Private Van Kyp?"

"Yes, sir."

"The one in whose behalf he was about to make application."

Ridge again answered in the affirmative.

"Colonel, I believe we want this young man."

"I believe we do," replied Colonel Wood. Then, to Ridge, he added: "If you can pass a satisfactory physical examination, I know of no reason why you should not be permitted to join this command. I want you to understand, though, that every man admitted to it is chosen solely for personal merit, and not through friendship or any influence, political or otherwise, that he may possess. Now you may take that horse to the picket-line, see that it is properly cared for, and report at my quarters in half an hour."

Without uttering a word in reply, but again saluting, Ridge rode away happier than he had ever been in his life, and prouder even than when he had won the silver hurdles at Yokohama.

An hour later he had successfully passed his

physical examination, and was waiting, with a dozen other recruits, to be sworn into the military service of the United States. To these men came Lieutenant-Colonel Roosevelt, who had just resigned the Assistant-Secretaryship of the Navy in order to join the front rank of those who were to fight his country's battles. To them he said: "Gentlemen, you have reached the last point. If any one of you does not mean business, let him say so now. In a few minutes more it will be too late to back out. Once in, you must see the thing through, performing without flinching whatever duty is assigned to you, regardless of its difficulty or danger. If it be garrison duty, you must attend to it; if meeting the fever, you must be willing; if it is the hardest kind of fighting, you must be anxious for it. You must know how to ride, how to shoot, and how to live in the open, lacking all the luxuries and often the necessities of life. No matter what comes, you must not squeal. Remember, above everything, that absolute obedience to every command is your first lesson. Now think it over, and if any man wishes to withdraw, he will be gladly excused, for hundreds stand ready to take his place."

Did any of those young men accept this chance to escape the dangers and privations, the hardships and sufferings, awaiting them? Not one, but all joined in an eager rivalry to first take the oath of allegiance and obedience, and sign the regimental roll.

As it happened, this honor fell to Ridge Norris,

and a few minutes later he passed out of the building an enlisted soldier of the United States, a private in its first regiment of volunteer cavalry, and ordered to report to the first sergeant of Troop "K"—Rollo Van Kyp's troop, he remembered with pleasure. "Poor old boy! how I wish I could see him and tell him of my good luck!" he reflected. "Wonder how long he will be kept in that beastly guard-house?"

At the moment our young trooper was passing headquarters, and even as this thought came into his mind, he was bidden by Colonel Wood to deliver a written order to the corporal of the guard. "It is for the release from arrest of your friend Van Kyp," explained the colonel, kindly, "and you may tell him that it was obtained through the intercession of Lieutenant-Colonel Roosevelt."

With a light heart Ridge hastened to perform this first act of his military service; and not long afterwards he and Rollo were happily engaged, under the supervision of Sergeant Higgins, in erecting the little dog-tent that they were to occupy in company, and settling their scanty belongings within its narrow limits. When this was finally accomplished to their satisfaction, they went to the picket-line to visit the pretty and high-spirited mare that had been the immediate cause of Ridge's good fortune.

"Isn't she a beauty?" he exclaimed, walking directly up to the mare, and throwing an arm about her neck, a caress to which the animal submitted with evident pleasure.

"Yes," admitted Rollo, hesitatingly, as he stepped nimbly aside to avoid a snap of white teeth. "I suppose she is, but she seems awfully vicious, and I can't say that she is exactly the style of horse that I most admire. Tell you what I'll do, Norris. I'll give her to you, seeing that you and she seem to hit it off so well. You've won her by rights, anyhow."

Ridge's face flushed. He already loved the mare, and longed to own her, but his pride forbade him to accept so valuable a gift from one who was but little more than a stranger. So he said:

"Oh no! Thanks, awfully, old man, but I couldn't think of taking her in that way. If you don't mind, though, I'll buy the mare of you, gladly paying whatever you gave for her."

"Very good," replied Rollo, who imagined Ridge to be quite well off, and to whom any question of money was of slight consequence. "I paid an even hundred dollars for her with saddle and bridle thrown in, and if you won't accept her as a gift, you may have her for that sum."

"Done," said Ridge, "and here's your money." With this he pulled from his pocket the roll of bills that his father, bidding him not to spend them recklessly, had thrust into his hand on parting, and which until now he had not found occasion to touch.

Although this left our young soldier penniless, he

did not for a moment regret the transaction by which he had gained possession of what he considered the very best mount in the whole regiment. He at once named the beautiful mare " Señorita," and upon her he lavished a wealth of affection that seemed to be fully reciprocated. While no one else could do anything with her, in Ridge's hands she gained a knowledge of cavalry tactics as readily as did her young master, and by her quick precision of movement when on drill or parade she was instrumental in raising him first to the grade of corporal, and then to that of sergeant, which was the rank he held three weeks later, on the eve of the Rough Riders' departure for Tampa.

In the mean time the days spent at San Antonio were full of active interest and hard work from morning reveille until the mellow trumpet-notes of taps. At the same time it was work mixed with a vast amount of harmless skylarking, in which both Ridge and Rollo took such active part as to win the liking of every member of their troop.

Each day heard the same anxious inquiry from a thousand tongues: "When shall we go to the front? Is the navy going to fight out this war without the army getting a show?"

"Be patient," counselled the wiser men, "and our chance will come. The powerful Spanish fleet under Admiral Cervera must first be located and rendered harmless, while the army must be licked into effective shape before it is allowed to fight."

They heard of the blockade by the navy of

Havana and other Cuban ports, of the apparently fruitless bombardment of San Juan in Porto Rico, and of the great gathering of troops and transports at Tampa. Finally came the welcome news that the dreaded Spanish fleet was safely bottled by Admiral Sampson in the narrow harbor of Santiago.

Then on the 29th of May, only a little more than one month after the declaration of war, came the welcome order to move to Tampa and the front. Instantly the camp presented a scene of wildest bustle and excitement. One hundred railway cars, in six long trains, awaited the Riders. The regiment was drawn up as if for parade.

"Forward, march!" ordered Colonel Wood.

"On to Cuba!" sang the trumpets.

And the "Terrors" yelled themselves hoarse at the prospect of being let loose.

## CHAPTER VI

### OFF FOR THE WAR

OF course Ridge had written home and informed his family of his whereabouts as soon as he found himself regularly enlisted with the Rough Riders. The news afforded Mr. Norris immense satisfaction, while Spence Cuthbert declared that if Ridge were her brother she should be proud of him.

"If that is said for my benefit," remarked Dulce, "you may rest assured that I am always proud of my brother. I must confess, though, that I should like it better if he were an officer; for, as I have never known any private soldiers, I can't imagine what they are like. It must be very unpleasant, though, to have to associate with them all the time. I wish Ridge had told us more about that Mr. Van Kyp who owns the car. Of course, though, one of his wealth and position must be an officer, a captain at the very least, and perhaps Ridge doesn't see much of him now."

Mrs. Norris was greatly disappointed to find that all her efforts in her son's behalf had been wasted. That he should have deliberately chosen to become a "common soldier," as she expressed it, instead of accepting the commission offered him, was beyond her comprehension. She mourned and puzzled over this until the arrival of Ridge's next letter, which conveyed the gratifying intelligence that, having been made a corporal, he was now an officer. She did not know what a corporal was, but that Ridge had risen above the ranks of "common soldiers" was sufficient, and from that moment the fond mother began to speak with pride of her son, who was an officer in the cavalry.

At length the quiet household was thrown into a flutter of excitement by the receipt of a telegram, which read:

"Have again been promoted. Regiment ordered to Tampa. Leave to-day. Meet us at Algiers, if possible."

Mr. Norris hurried into the city to consult railway officials concerning the movements of the regiment, and found that the train bearing his son's troop would pass through the city on the morrow.

Early the next morning, therefore, he escorted his wife and the girls across the Mississippi, where, in the forlorn little town of Algiers, they awaited as patiently as might be the coming of their soldier boy. The mother's anxiety to meet her son was almost equalled by her desire to see how handsome he would look in an officer's uniform. Concerning this she had formed a mental picture of epaulettes, gold lace, brass buttons, plumes, and a sword; for had she not seen army officers in Paris?

The two girls discussed as to whether or not

Ridge was now travelling in the same luxurious private car that had borne him to San Antonio. Spence thought not, but Dulce believed he would be. "Of course if Ridge was still a private I don't suppose it would be good form for *Captain* Van Kyp to invite him," she said; "but now that he is an officer, and perhaps even of equal rank, I can't imagine any reason why they should not travel together as they did before."

There was no reason, and the joint proprietors of the little dog-tent, of which, when in marching order, each carried one-half, were travelling together on terms of perfect equality, as was discovered a little later, when the long train, thickly coated with dust and cinders, rumbled heavily into the station. Heads protruded from every window of the crowded coaches, and hundreds of eyes gazed approvingly at the pretty girls who were anxiously looking for a private car, while trying not to blush at the very audible compliments by which they were greeted.

Suddenly they heard the familiar voice. "Mother! Father! Girls!" it called, and turning quickly in that direction, they discovered the object of their search. Sun-browned and dust-begrimed, his face streaked by rivulets of perspiration, wearing a disreputable-looking felt hat and a coarse blue flannel shirt, open at the throat, their boy, beaming with delight, was eagerly beckoning to them. Two other cinder-hued faces were attempting to share the window with him, but with only partial success.

The car doors were guarded, and no one was allowed to pass either in or out until the train was safely on the great boat that was to transfer it across the river. There the turbulent stream of humanity was permitted to burst forth, and in another moment a stalwart young soldier, who seemed to have broadened by inches since she last saw him, had flung his arms about Mrs. Norris's neck. Then he shook hands with his father and kissed both the girls, at which Spence Cuthbert blushed more furiously than ever.

A score of young fellows, all as grimy as Ridge, and all wearing the same uniform, watched this performance curiously, and now the latter began to present them.

"This is First Sergeant Higgins, mother, of our troop, and Mr. Gridley, and Mr. Pine of North Dakota. Dulce, allow me to introduce my tentmate, Mr. Van Kyp."

So he rattled off name after name, until the poor girls were thoroughly bewildered, and could not tell which belonged to whom, especially, as Dulce said, when they all looked exactly alike in those absurd hats, horrid flannel shirts, and ridiculous leggings.

Rollo Van Kyp was the only one of whose name and personality she felt certain, which is probably the reason she allowed that persuasive young trooper to escort her to the forward deck of the boat, where they remained until the river was almost crossed. After a while Ridge and Spence also strolled off together, ostensibly to find Dulce and Rollo, though they did not succeed until the farther shore was nearly reached, when all four came back together.

Rollo Van Kip had lost his hat, while Dulce held tightly in one daintily gloved hand a curious-looking package done up in newspaper. At the same time Spence Cuthbert blushed whenever something in the pocket of her gown gave forth a metallic jingle, and glanced furtively about to see if any one else had heard it.

A few days later Dulce appeared in a new riding-hat, which at once attracted the admiration and envy of all her girl friends. At the same time it was a very common affair, exactly like those worn by Uncle Sam's soldier boys, and on its front was rudely traced in lead pencil the words, "Troop K, Roosevelt's Rough Riders." In fact, it was one of the very hats that Dulce herself had recently designated as "absurd."

About the same time that Miss Norris appeared wearing a trooper's hat her friend Miss Cuthbert decorated the front of her riding-jacket with brass buttons. When Sergeant Norris sharply reprimanded Private Van Kyp for losing his hat, Rollo answered that he considered himself perfectly excusable for so doing, since in a breeze strong enough to blow the buttons off a sergeant's blouse a hat stood no show to remain on its owner's head, whereupon the other abruptly changed the subject.

In the mean time Mrs. Norris, who had recognized among the names of the young men presented to her those of some of the best-known families of the country, was surrounded by a group of Ridge's friends, who, as they all wore the same uniform that he did, she imagined must also be officers. So she delighted their hearts and rose high in their estimation by treating them with great cordiality, and calling them indiscriminately major, captain, or whatever military title happened on the end of her tongue. This she did until her husband appeared on the scene with Lieutenant-Colonel Roosevelt, whom he had known in Washington. The moment the fond mother discovered this gentleman to be her son's superior officer, she neglected every one else to ply him with questions.

"Did he think her boy would make a fine soldier? Was Ridge really an officer? If so, what was his rank, and why did he not wear a more distinctive uniform? Did *General* Roosevelt believe there would be any fighting, and if there was, would he not order Ridge to remain in the safest places?"

To all of these questions the Lieutenant-Colonel managed to return most satisfactory answers. He thought Ridge was in a fair way to make a most excellent soldier, seeing that he had already gained the rank of sergeant, which was very rapid promotion, considering the short time the young man had been in the service. As to his uniform, he now wore that especially designed for active campaigning, which Mrs. Norris must know was much less showy than one that would be donned for dress parades in time of peace. Yes, he fancied there might be a little fighting, in which case he meditated giving Ridge a place behind Sergeant Borrowe's dynamite gun, where he would be as safe as in any other position on the whole firing line.

Not only was Mrs. Norris greatly comforted by these kindly assurances, but she received further evidence that her boy was indeed an officer entitled to command and be obeyed when the troopers were ordered to re-enter the cars, for she heard him say:

"Come, boys, tumble in lively! Now, Rollo, get a move on."

Certainly an officer to whom even *Captain* Van Kyp yielded obedience must be of exalted rank.

There was some delay in starting the train, which was taken advantage of by Mr. Norris to disappear, only to return a few minutes later, followed by a porter bearing a great basket of fruit. This was given to Ridge for distribution among his friends. Spence Cuthbert also shyly handed him a box of choice candies, which she had carried all this time; but Dulce, seeing her brother thus well provided, gave her box to Rollo Van Kyp—a proceeding that filled the young millionaire with delight, and caused him to be furiously envied by every other man in the car.

Finally the heavy train began slowly to pull out, its occupants raised a mighty cheer, the trumpeters sounded their liveliest quickstep, and those left behind, waving their handkerchiefs and shouting words of farewell, felt their eyes fill with sudden tears. Until this moment the war had been merely a subject for careless discussion, a thing remote from them, and only affecting far-away people. Now it was real and terrible. Their nearest and dearest was concerned in it. They had witnessed the going of those who might never return. From that moment it was their war.

On Thursday, June 2d, with their long, dusty journey ended, the last of the Rough Riders reached Tampa, hot and weary, but in good spirits, and eager to be sent at once to the front. They found 25,000 troops, cavalry, infantry, and artillery, most of them regulars, already encamped in the sandy pine barrens surrounding the little city, and took their place among them.

At Port Tampa, nine miles away, lay the fleet of transports provided to carry them to Cuba. Here they had lain for many days. Here the army had waited for weeks, sweltering in the pitiless heat, suffering the discomforts of a campaign without its stimulant of excitement, impatient of delay, and sick with repeated disappointments. The regulars were ready for service; the volunteers thought they were, but knew better a few weeks later. Time and again orders for embarkation were received, only to be revoked upon rumors of ghostly warships reported off some distant portion of the coast. Spain was playing her old game of *mañana* at the expense of the Americans, and inducing her powerful enemy to refrain from striking a blow by means of terrifying rumors skilfully circulated through the so-called "yellow journals" of the great American cities, which readily published any falsehood that provided a sensation. At length, however, the last bogie appeared to be laid, and one week after the Riders reached Tampa a rumor of an immediate departure, more definite than any that had preceded it, flashed through the great camp: "Everything is ready, and to-morrow we shall surely embark for Santiago."

## CHAPTER VII

THE STORY OF HOBSON AND THE *MERRIMAC*

ONLY half the regiment was to go, and no horses could be taken, except a few belonging to officers. The capacity of the transports was limited, and though troops were packed into them like sardines into a can, there was only room for 15,000 men, together with a few horses, a pack-train of mules, four light batteries, and two of siege-guns. So, thousands of soldiers, heartbroken by disappointment, and very many things important to the success of a campaign, were to be left behind.

Two dismounted squadrons of the Rough Riders were chosen to accompany the expedition, which, with the exception of themselves and two regiments of volunteer infantry, was composed of regulars; and, to the great joy of Ridge and his immediate friends, their troop was among those thus selected. But their joy was dimmed by being dismounted, and Ridge almost wept when obliged to part with his beloved mare.

However, as Rollo philosophically remarked, "Everything goes in time of war, or rather most everything does, and what can't go must be left behind."

Some ve hundred of the horseless riders were piled into a train of empty coal-cars, each man carrying on his person in blanket roll and haversack whatever baggage he was allowed to take, and they were rattled noisily away to Port Tampa, where, after much vexatious delay, they finally boarded the transport *Yucatan*, and felt that they were fairly off for Cuba.

But not yet. Again came a rumor of strange war-ships hovering off the coast, and with it a frightened but imperative order from Washington to *wait*. So they waited in the broiling heat, crowded almost to suffocation in narrow spaces — men delicately reared and used to every luxury, men who had never before breathed any but the pure air of mountain or boundless plain — and their only growl was at the delay that kept them from going to where conditions would be even worse. They ate their coarse food whenever and wherever they could get it, drank tepid water from tin cups that were equally available for soup or coffee, and laughed at their discomforts. "But why don't they let us go?" was the constant cry heard on all sides at all hours.

During this most tedious of all their waitings, only one thing of real interest happened. They had heard of the daring exploit of Naval Lieutenant Richmond Pearson Hobson, who, on the night of June 3d, had sunk the big coal-steamer *Merrimac* in the narrowest part of Santiago Harbor, in the hope of thus preventing the escape of Admiral

Cervera's bottled fleet, and they had exulted over this latest example of dauntless American heroism, but none of the details had yet reached them.

On one of their waiting days a swift steam-yacht, now an armed government despatch-boat, dashed into Tampa Bay, and dropped anchor near the *Yucatan*. Rumor immediately had it that she was from the blockading fleet of Santiago, and every eye was turned upon her with interest. A small boat carried her commanding officer ashore, and while he was gone another brought one of her juniors, Ensign Dick Comly, to visit his only brother, who was a Rough Rider. The *Speedy* had just come from Santiago, and of course Ensign Comly knew all about Hobson. Would he tell the story of the *Merrimac?* Certainly he would, and so a few minutes after his arrival the naval man was relating the thrilling tale as follows:

"I don't suppose many of you fellows ever heard of Hobson before this, but every one in the navy knew of him long ago. He is from Alabama, was the youngest man in the Naval Academy class of '89, graduated number 2, was sent abroad to study naval architecture, and, upon returning to this country, was given the rank of Assistant Naval Constructor. At the beginning of this war he was one of the instructors at Annapolis, but immediately applied for active duty, and was assigned to the *New York*.

"When Victor Blue, of the *Suwanee*, had proved beyond a doubt by going ashore and counting them that all of Cervera's ships were in Santiago Harbor,

Hobson conceived the plan of keeping them there by taking in a ship and sinking it across the channel. Of course it was a perfectly useless thing to do, for Sampson's fleet is powerful enough to lick the stuffing out of the whole Spanish navy, if only it could get the chance. However, the notion took with the Admiral, and Hobson was told to go ahead.

"He selected the collier *Merrimac*, a big iron steamer 300 feet long, stripped her of all valuable movables, and fastened a lot of torpedoes to her bottom. Each one of these was sufficiently powerful to sink the ship, and all were connected by wires with a button on the bridge. Hobson's plan was to steam into the channel at full speed, regardless of mines or batteries, and anchor his ship across the narrowest part of the channel. There he proposed to blow her up and sink her. What was to become of himself and the half dozen men who were to go with him I don't know, and don't suppose he cared.

"At the same time there was some provision made for escape in case any of them survived the blowing up of their ship. They carried one small dingy along, and an old life-raft was left on board. A steam-launch from the *New York* was to follow them close in under the batteries, and lie there so long as there was a chance of picking any of them up, or until driven off. Cadets Palmer and Powell, each eager to go on this service, drew lots to see which should command the launch, and luck favored the latter.

"When it was known that six men were wanted to accompany Hobson to almost certain death, four thousand volunteered, and three thousand nine hundred and ninety-four were mightily disappointed when the other six were chosen."

"I should have felt just as they did if I had been left in camp," said Ridge, who was following this story with eager interest.

"Me too," replied Rollo Van Kyp, to whom the remark was addressed.

"The worst of it was," continued the Ensign, "that those fellows didn't get to go, after all, for when they had put in twenty-four hours of hard work on the *Merrimac*, with no sleep and but little to eat, only kept up by the keenest kind of excitement, it was decided to postpone the attempt until the following night. At the same time the Admiral, fearing the nerve of the men would be shaken by so long a strain, ordered them back to their ships, with thanks for their devotion to the service, and selected six others to take their places. The poor fellows were so broken up by this that some of them cried like babies."

"It was as bad as though we should be ordered to remain behind now," said Ridge.

"Yes," answered Rollo. "But that would be more than I could bear. I'd mutiny and refuse to go ashore. Wouldn't you?"

"I should certainly feel like it," laughed the former. "But orders are orders, and we have sworn to obey them, you know. At the same time there's no cause for worry. We are certain to go if any one does."

"Yes, me and Teddy—" began Rollo, but Ridge silenced him that they might hear the continuation of the Ensign's story.

"At three o'clock on Friday morning, the 3d," resumed Comly, "the *Merrimac* left the fleet and steamed in towards Santiago entrance. On board, besides Hobson and his six chosen men, was one other, a coxswain of the *New York*, who had helped prepare the collier for her fate, and at the last moment stowed himself away in her hold for the sake of sharing it.

"With Hobson on the bridge, two men at the wheel, two in the engine-room, two stoking, and one forward ready to cut away the anchor, the doomed ship entered the narrow water-way and passed the outer line of mines in safety. Then the Spaniards discovered her, and from the way they let loose they must have thought the whole American fleet was trying to force the passage. In an instant she was the focus for a perfect cyclone of shot and shell from every gun that could be brought to bear, on both sides of the channel.

"It was like rushing into the very jaws of hell, with mines exploding all about her, solid shot and bursting shells tearing at her vitals, and a cloud of Mauser bullets buzzing like hornets across her deck. How she lived to get where she was wanted is a mystery; but she did, and they sunk her just inside the Estrella battery. At the last they could not steer her, because her rudder was knocked away. So they anchored, waited as cool as cucumbers for the tide to swing her into position, opened all their sea-valves, touched off their torpedoes, and blew her up.

"So far everything had worked to perfection. The seven men, still unhurt, were well aft, where Hobson joined them the moment he had pressed the button; but now their troubles began. The dingy in which they had hoped to escape had been shot to pieces, and they dared not try to get their raft overboard, for the growing light would have revealed their movements, and they would have been a target for every gunner and rifleman within range. So they could only lie flat on deck and wait for something to happen. A little after daybreak the ship sank so low and with such a list that the raft slipped into the water and floated of its own accord. On this all of them, including two had been wounded by flying splinters, rolled overboard after it, caught hold of the clumsy old float, and tried to swim it out to where Powell could pick them up. They had only gained a few yards when a steam-launch coming from the harbor bore down on them. Some marines in the bow were about to open fire, when Hobson sang out, ' Is there any officer on board that launch entitled to receive the surrender of prisoners of war?'

"'Yes, señor, there is,' answered a voice, which also ordered the marines not to fire, and I'll be blowed if Admiral Cervera himself didn't stick his head out from under the awning. The old fellow was as nice as pie to Hobson and his men, told them they had done a fine thing, took them back to his ship, fed them, fitted them out with dry clothing, and then sent Captain Oviedo, his chief of staff, out to the *New York*, under a flag of truce, to report that the *Merrimac's* crew, though prisoners, were alive and well. He also offered to carry back any message or supplies the American Admiral might choose to send them. Didn't every soul in that fleet yell when the signal of Hobson's safety was made? Well, I should rather say we did. I only hope old Cervera will fall into our hands some day, so that we can show him how we appreciate his decency."

"Three cheers for the Spanish Admiral right now!" shouted Ridge, and the yell that instantly rose from the deck of the *Yucatan* in reply was heard on shore for a mile inland.

The noise had barely subsided when a voice called for Sergeant Norris.

"Here I am. Who wants me?" replied Ridge, inquiringly.

"Take your belongings ashore, sir, and report back at camp immediately," was the startling response, delivered in the form of an order by Major Herman Dodley, who was now on the staff of the commanding general. "I have a boat in waiting. If you are ready within two minutes I will set you ashore. Otherwise you will suffer the consequences of your own delay," added the Major, who, while on duty at Port Tampa, had received by telegraph the orders he was now carrying out.

## CHAPTER VIII

#### CHARGED WITH A SECRET MISSION

HAVING ascertained from the captain of his troop that the order brought by Major Dodley was one that must be obeyed, Ridge went below with a very heavy heart to collect his scanty possessions. As he did so his thoughts were full of bitterness. Why should any one be sent back to that hateful camp, and for what reason had he been singled out from all his fellows? It looked as though he were being disgraced, or at least chosen for some duty that would keep him from going to Cuba, which would be almost as bad. At the same time he could not imagine what he had done to incur the displeasure of his superiors. It was all a mystery, and a decidedly unpleasant one. That the order should come through Dodley, too, whom he particularly disliked, was adding insult to injury.

"I'd rather swim ashore than go with that man!" he exclaimed to Rollo Van Kyp, who, full of sympathy, and genuinely distressed at the prospect of their separation, had gone below with him. Ridge had told his chum all about Dodley, whom they had discovered lounging on a breezy veranda of the great

Tampa Bay hotel a few days before, so that now the latter fully comprehended his feelings.

"It's a beastly shame!" cried Rollo; "or rather it's two beastly shames, and if you say so, old man, we'll just quietly chuck that Major fellow overboard, so that you can have his boat all to yourself. Then, instead of going ashore, you head down the bay for some place where you can hide until we come along and pick you up."

"That's a great scheme," replied Ridge, with a sorrowful little smile, "but I am afraid it wouldn't work, and so there is nothing left for me but submission to the inevitable. I do hate to go with Dodley, though."

Just here Ensign Comly appeared on the scene with his brother, whom he was bidding farewell.

"I say, Comly!" cried Rollo, who knew him, "why can't you set my friend Norris here ashore? It wouldn't be much out of your way, would it?"

"Not at all," answered the ensign, courteously. "And I should be pleased to accommodate any friend of yours. I must go at once, though; so, if Mr. Norris will come on deck—"

"Oh, but that won't do," interrupted Van Kyp. "He must get off the ship without any one on deck seeing him." With this he explained the situation to the ensign, who readily grasped it, and said:

"All right. I'll run my boat in under this sideport, and he can drop out of it if the sentry will let him pass."

Of course the guard at the wide freight port left

open for a better circulation of air between decks would allow Ridge to pass, for he was one of their own troop, and knew that the sergeant had been ordered ashore. To give him further assurance that everything was all right, Ridge said:

"It is my duty, you know, to go in the first boat that offers, since Major Dodley undoubtedly left some time since. He said he would only wait two minutes, and as that was fully five minutes ago, he ought to be ashore by now."

Thus it happened that while the messenger who had been ordered to fetch Sergeant Norris of the Rough Riders was still fuming over the unpardonable delay of the trooper, and threatening all sorts of unpleasant things for him when he did appear, Ridge gained the railroad wharf without being observed from the deck of the transport. There, finding an empty train just starting for Tampa, he was able to present himself in camp half an hour later. From it he was sent to headquarters, with orders to report to Lieutenant-Colonel Roosevelt, who had come ashore early that morning. This Ridge hastened to do, without waiting to answer any of the eager questions showered upon him by his recent comrades of the camp.

At the hotel occupied as headquarters an orderly conducted him to the office of the commanding general, where, upon admittance, he found himself not only in the presence of his own superior officer, but of a group of distinguished looking men in uniform, who, as he afterwards discovered, were Generals Miles, Shafter, Lee, and Lawton, and Lieutenant Boldwood of the navy, now in command of the despatch boat *Speedy*, recently arrived.

"General," said Lieutenant-Colonel Roosevelt, addressing the commander-in-chief, "this is Sergeant Norris of my regiment, the man whom I recommended for your purpose, and for whom you sent less than an hour ago."

"Where were you when ordered to report here?" asked General Miles, turning abruptly to Ridge.

"On board the transport *Yucatan*, lying off Port Tampa, sir."

"Then you are one of the few men whom I have discovered among our volunteers who have learned the lesson of *prompt* obedience," remarked the general, with a slight scowl on his still handsome though deeply lined face.

"Umph!" snorted General Shafter, who was a big man, weighing about three hundred pounds, and whose hair was sadly rumpled, as though by much perplexity.

General Lee, also a large, fine-looking man, smiled approvingly at the prompt young trooper, while General "Iron" Lawton, spare of figure and with a reputation as a fighter, gave him a penetrating glance, that Ridge knew had indelibly fixed his face upon the soldier's memory. The naval man also regarded him with interest, and our hero, greatly confused at being thus observed, was relieved to have General Miles proceed to question him further.

"I understand that you speak Spanish like a native."

"I do, sir."

"Have you ever been in Cuba?"

"No, sir"

"Or travelled in Spain?"

"Yes, sir."

"Acquainted with its principal cities?"

"I am, sir," replied Ridge, wondering in what direction these questions were tending.

"Are you willing to encounter great risks and undergo great hardships in your country's service?"

"Certainly I am, sir," answered the young trooper, with flushed face, for he began to suspect that some more important duty was to be required of him than simply remaining in camp.

"In that case I am going to offer you the chance of winning your country's gratitude, and possibly with it an ignominious death. It is deemed imperative that some one intrusted with grave secrets should immediately set forth on an important mission to Cuba. If his identity is discovered before the task is completed, his fate will undoubtedly be that of a spy. Knowing this fact, are you ready to undertake it?"

"I am, sir," was the decisive reply.

"Good! A commissioned officer was selected for this duty, but he is prevented by illness from performing it. You have been chosen to take his place on the recommendation of Colonel Roosevelt because of your knowledge of Spanish, your military record, and because you are a native-born American. I could have found plenty of Cubans to undertake the mission, and possibly one of them would have carried it to a satisfactory ending, but I wanted an American."

"Plain North American Yankee," growled General Shafter.

"As you know," continued General Miles, "a powerful expedition is about to leave this place for Cuba. Very few persons have any idea where it is to land; but you must know that in about ten days from now it will appear off Daiquiri, some twelve miles east of Santiago, in which city I want you to be at that time. You will sail to-night in the despatch-boat *Speedy*, of which this gentleman, Lieutenant Boldwood, is the commander. Within three days he will land you on the northern coast of the province of Santiago. During the following week I want you to visit the Spanish commanders at Holguin, Jiguani, and Santiago, to all of whom you will bear what purport to be important despatches from Señor Carranza, chief of the Spanish secret service in North America, whose headquarters are in Montreal.

"You will represent yourself to be José Remelio, one of the clerks attached to the recent Spanish Legation at Washington. You will estimate the strength and condition of the Spanish forces in the province. Also, you will meet as many of the insurgent leaders as possible, inform them of the coming of our expedition, and impress upon them the necessity of intercepting supplies or re-inforcements for Santiago. For the sake of appearances, I authorize you to assume any military rank up to that of Captain you may deem advisable. You will also be given the secret countersign of the Cuban Junta, which will secure for you good treatment among all Cubans of intelligence."

"His best safeguard among Cubans should be that he is an American soldier," suggested General Lawton.

"You will perceive," continued General Miles, "that I have laid out a vast amount of work for you to perform in a very short time; but you will be provided with plenty of money, and by procuring a good horse as soon as possible after landing I believe you can accomplish it. I hope you will be able to reach Santiago and gain a knoweldge of its defences; but no matter where you are, when you hear that our army has landed, make your way to it with all speed, and report immediately to the commanding general. Is all this clear? and have you anything to suggest?"

"Your instructions are perfectly clear, sir," replied Ridge, his voice trembling with excitement, "and I only want to suggest that instead of depending upon Cuban horses for transportation across the island, I be allowed to take my own from here."

"Are you sure that your horse is enough better than those of the island to warrant carrying it to such a distance?"

"I can vouch for that, General," interposed Lieutenant-Colonel Roosevelt. "Sergeant Norris has one of the very best horses in our regiment, and one that has developed almost human intelligence under his training."

"No one realizes the value of a reliable horse in times of danger better than I," rejoined General Miles. "I wonder, though, if it will be possible to carry one on the *Speedy?*"

"I believe we can manage it, General," said Lieutenant Boldwood.

"Very, well, then, you may take your own horse. How will you get it to the port?"

"I think the simplest and probably the quickest way will be to ride her, sir."

"Then do so with all haste, for I want the *Speedy* to sail this very evening, and within two hours, if possible. You will receive your despatches, funds, and promised countersign after you get on board. Good-bye. Good luck to you, and remember that your proposed movements must be kept absolutely secret outside of this room."

Ridge had barely taken his departure after shaking hands with the several generals, who rose to bid him farewell, when a telegraph message was handed to General Shafter. He read it with perplexity, studied it for a few moments, and then burst into a roar of laughter. It was from his aide, Major Dodley, had been sent from Port Tampa, and read as follows:

"I charge Sergeant Norris of Rough Riders with

contempt, disobedience of orders, and desertion. Saw him aboard transport, and delivered your order, whereupon he disappeared. Have searched ship without discovering trace of him. He has undoubtedly deserted."

"Some persons are fools occasionally," remarked the big General, "while others are never anything else. I don't think Dodley belongs to the former class."

## CHAPTER IX

### HERMAN DODLEY INTERPOSES DIFFICULTIES

AFTER leaving headquarters, and while making his way back to camp, our hero was in a state of hardly-to-be-repressed excitement. Was one of his age and limited experience ever intrusted with so important a mission? He did not believe it possible, and was so filled with pride that it seemed as though every person he passed ought to regard him with respectful interest. As one after another only glanced at him carelessly or failed to notice him at all, he wondered at their stupidity, and felt like compelling their attention by proclaiming his great secret.

At camp the situation was even more aggravating, for every one was so intent on his own affairs or so unhappy at being left behind that Ridge found himself barely noticed. Several questioned him concerning his return, and one asked if the whole regiment was ordered back.

"Not that I know of," answered Ridge. "I believe I am the only one thus far."

"Well, I'm glad you have been sent to the rear, and only wish all the others were as well, for it's a beastly outrage that some should be taken and others left. Just as if we weren't as good as any of them!" was the bitter comment.

Without reply, Ridge turned towards the place where he had left his blanket roll, only to encounter another shock to his recent pride. An officer met him.

"Hello! What troop do you belong to?" he asked, suspiciously.

"Troop K, sir," answered Ridge, saluting.

"I thought so. What are you doing here?"

"I was ordered ashore."

"Humph! Without any reason at all, I suppose."

Ridge remained silent.

"Oh, well, if you don't choose to tell why you are in disgrace you needn't, but you may report to the cook of the officers' mess, who is in need of an assistant."

Here was a dilemma. Ridge could not, of course, obey this order, since every moment was precious. To disobey would cause his arrest and detention in the guard-house. Nor could he inform even this officer of the secret mission on which he was engaged. At that moment evening stable-call was sounded, and a happy inspiration came to his relief.

"Very well, sir," he answered, turning as if to obey the order. Then he added, "May I look after my horse first?"

"I suppose so," replied the officer. "Only be quick about it, for the cook is badly in need of some one to help him."

So, without making a further attempt to recover his personal belongings, Ridge hastened to the picket-line, where Señorita manifested most extravagant joy at again seeing her young master.

"Is that your horse?" inquired the non-commissioned officer in charge of the stable guard.

Upon Ridge acknowledging that the mare was his, the other continued:

"Well, I'm mighty glad you've come to look after her, for she has nearly killed two men already, and we were just wondering whether we should kill her or turn her loose. Now you'd better take her to water."

"May I put on a saddle and bridle?" inquired Ridge.

"Of course not. Who ever heard of riding a cavalry horse to water any way but bareback?"

So the young trooper was obliged to set forth on his great undertaking without equipment of any kind. In his joy at finding himself once more in possession of his beloved "Rita," this did not trouble him; and untying the mare's halter, he leaped to her back. In an instant they were dashing off at full speed, followed by jeers from all who witnessed the proceeding, and who imagined the mare to be running away with her present rider, as she had with every other who had attempted to take her to water during her master's absence.

The camp was quickly left behind, and knowing his general direction, Ridge soon found himself on the road to Port Tampa. It was a hard ride to make without saddle or bridle, and long before the welcome lights marking the mile-long pier of the port came into view the young soldier was aching in every bone. The dim road through the solemn pines was so heavy with sand that it took even fleet-footed Rita more than an hour to cover the distance, and night had closed in before their destination was reached.

It was with many misgivings that Ridge rode out on the long pier, which, never intended for the use of horses or wagons, carried only a sidewalk for pedestrians beside its railway-track, for Rita regarded locomotives with the utmost terror. Still, he believed he must go to the extreme outer end, where the big steamers lay, and where he hoped to find either the *Speedy* herself or some one from her to direct his movements. Half-way out he discovered a train coming directly towards them, and, to avoid it, turned his mare on to the platform that served as front yard to the pretty little inn that was here built over the water.

At this moment a figure in white duck approached him. It was Ensign Comly of the *Speedy*.

"You are the very man I was sent to look for!" he cried. "I thought you might be coming out here, and so was on my way to head you off and turn you back. You see, the end of the pier is so crowded that our craft can't lie alongside. So Captain Boldwood got hold of a small scow, which he has sent in to shore, towed by one of our boats, to take you off. We'll just about meet it if we hurry."

By this time the unusual sight of a horse in that place had aroused much curiosity among the guests of the inn, who came out to see what was going on. Among them was an army officer, who uttered an exclamation the moment his eyes rested on Ridge standing in the glow of an electric light. Stepping quickly up to him, he placed a heavy hand on the young trooper's shoulder, and said, in a harsh voice:

"I arrest you, sir, and order you to come at once with me to my camp on shore, where a guard-house awaits you."

"On what charge am I arrested?" asked Ridge, calmly, turning, and looking Major Herman Dodley full in the face.

"On the several charges of contempt for an officer, disobedience of orders, and desertion," was the startling reply.

"Very well, sir, I'll go with you," said Ridge, "seeing that I was going in that direction anyhow."

"But—" remonstrated Ensign Comly.

"Who are you, sir? And what have you to say regarding this business?" demanded the Major, fiercely, at the same time drawing and cocking his revolver.

"Only a United States officer."

"Then, in the name of the United States, I call upon you to assist me in carrying this deserter to a place of security," shouted the Major, in theatrical tones.

"Pretend to agree," said Ridge, in a low voice, heard only by Comly.

"All right, Major, I'll see the thing through," agreed the navy man; "though I must protest that it is wholly out of my line of business."

With this the three set forth, Ridge leading Rita, and the officers walking on either side of him. For some distance they proceeded in a silence that was finally broken by the sound of oars, apparently close to the pier, which touched land but a short distance ahead. At the same time a train of cars came thundering over the hollow structure behind them, causing the mare to plunge violently in a terrified effort to escape.

"Now is your chance!" whispered Comly.

Quick to take the hint, Ridge flung himself on the animal's back and dashed away, followed by a harmless bullet from Herman Dodley's revolver.

Ere he could fire another shot the naval man snatched away the weapon, flung it into the sea, and started on a run after the disappearing horseman. As he ran he shouted: "Look out for that horse, you in the boat, and get it aboard lively! Do you understand?"

"Ay, ay, sir," came a cheery answer from out of the darkness.

Behind the Ensign ran Major Dodley, swearing, and also shouting:

"Corporal of the guard! Turn out the guard! Quick! This way!"

Then all other sounds were drowned in the roar of the passing train. When it subsided a confused struggle between a dark mass and a number of dimly seen white forms was going on in the shallow water. Several sailors were lifting Señorita bodily into a little flat-bottomed boat, and two young men in soaked uniforms were aiding them. Then, as two boats, one in tow of the other, began to move away, a squad of soldiers with muskets in their hands came running down to the beach.

"Fire!" commanded Herman Dodley, beside himself with rage. "Fire at that boat. A deserter is escaping in it."

"Don't you dare fire!" came back in a stern tone from the darkness. "This is a boat from a United States man-of-war, commanded by an officer in the discharge of his duty."

The bewildered soldiers hesitated, and then, in compliance with repeated orders, coupled with threats, from their Major, fired a few harmless shots in the air, after which they returned to camp. There Herman Dodley prepared another telegraphic report for General Shafter, that aroused that irascible warrior to profanity, and resulted in the speedy transference of his offending aide to New Orleans on recruiting service.

So our hero was at length fairly started on his momentous mission, with its secret yet undivulged. As the *Speedy*, with the bewildered Señorita and her young master safely on board, slipped swiftly past the great transport *Yucatan*, Ridge, shivering in his wet clothing, said to Ensign Comly, who also shivered, "How I wish I could call out and tell Rollo all about it!"

"Yes, wouldn't it make him open his eyes? But you can't, so let's go below for something dry."

CHAPTER X

ON THE CUBAN BLOCKADE

TWELVE hours after leaving Tampa Bay the swift despatch-boat on which Ridge Norris was a passenger entered the northwest passage of Key West Harbor, and was headed towards the quaint island city that had been brought into such sudden prominence by the war. The port was filled with United States cruisers, gun-boats, yachts converted into torpedo-boat destroyers, Government hospital-ships, and others flying the flag of the Red Cross Society, transports, colliers, supply-ships, water-boats, and a huddle of prizes — steamers and sailing-vessels captured off the Cuban coast. Amid these the *Speedy* slowly threaded her devious way to the Government dock.

The hot tropical-looking city, with palm-trees towering above its low-roofed houses, was filled to overflowing with soldiers, sailors, newspaper correspondents, refugees from Cuba, and a multitude of other persons, all attracted by its proximity to the seat of war. From every mast-head and prominent building the stars and stripes were flung to the breeze that swept in from the sea; while from more humble positions, but in even greater numbers, fluttered the flag of free Cuba. On every point commanding the harbor mouth batteries were being erected and great guns mounted. Bands played national airs, and one man-of-war enveloped in a cloud of white smoke was engaged in target-practice with her secondary battery. Every Government vessel in the harbor had on war paint of invisible lead color, not pretty, but most businesslike in appearance. All were also in fighting-trim, with topmasts lowered and every superfluity removed from their decks. The whole scene was of exciting interest, and Ridge gazed eagerly upon it as Ensign Comly pointed out its various features, with explanatory remarks.

There were several reasons why the *Speedy* should stop at Key West. One was that she might receive mail and despatches for the blockading fleet. Another was to procure a bale of hay and some corn for Señorita, since, in their hurried departure from Tampa, these had been forgotten, and thus far she had been fed on sea-biscuit. A third reason was that Ridge might procure a saddle and bridle, besides a few other necessary articles of outfit for his proposed trip.

He had already been furnished with his bogus despatches to Spanish commanders, every word of which he had carefully read, to see that they contained no compromising errors, and with a supply of money. Now he provided himself with a repeating-rifle in a water-proof case, a revolver, fifty rounds of ammunition for each, an India-rubber poncho, a small quantity of quinine, a phial of powerful cholera mixture, a stout sheath-knife, and a tin cup.

Within an hour the *Speedy* was again off, running out of the south channel, past the grim walls of old Fort Taylor, and a few miles farther on passing Sand Key light, which rises from a bit of coral reef barely lifted above the wash of a tranquil sea. At that time this was the most southerly point of United States territory. In the deep water just beyond Sand Key lay a great battle-ship, tugging sullenly at her pondrous anchors, and looking like some vast sea monster, uncouth and relentless.

From here it was eighty-five miles in a straight line to Havana, and within five hours Ridge was thrilled by the sight of a cloud-like speck that he knew marked the highlands of Cuba. Gradually the coast was revealed, then came the low-trailing smoke of ships on blockade as they patrolled wearily before the entrance to Havana Harbor, and after awhile the outlined cathedral spires of the city itself. There lay the wreck of the *Maine*, and there waited the Spanish army that Captain-General Blanco had sworn should yield its last drop of blood in resisting an invasion by the hated Yankees. There also the guns of time-blackened Morro sullenly faced the floating fortresses that only awaited a signal to engage them in deadly conflict.

Running close to Commodore Watson's flag-ship,

the *San Francisco*, the *Speedy* broke the tedious monotony of blockade by delivering an eagerly welcomed mail, with its wealth of news from the outside world. Then the saucy craft was off again, headed to the eastward. Matanzas and Cardenas, both under blockade, were passed during the night, and while off the latter place Dick Comly told Ridge the story of his classmate, Ensign Worth Bagley, who lost his life on board the torpedo-boat *Winslow*, in Cardenas Bay, on May 11th, or less than one month before, and who was the first American officer killed in the war.

"They only went in to find out who was there," began Comly, "the *Wilmington, Hudson*, and *Winslow*. The last, being of least draught, ran ahead, and got within range of some hidden batteries before she discovered them. She was turning to go out when they opened fire. In a minute the little ship was riddled by shot and shell. Her commander was wounded, her steering-gear had gone wrong, her engines were crippled, and she lay helpless. The *Hudson* ran up to tow her out of range, and poor old Bagley had just sung out for them to heave him a line, as the situation was getting rather too warm for comfort, when a bursting shell instantly killed him, together with four of the crew. In spite of the hot fire, the *Hudson* ran a line and brought out what was left of the *Winslow* and her company; but you'd better believe the little craft was a mighty sad-looking wreck. Hello! What's that?"

A string of colored signal-lights had flashed out for a moment directly ahead of the *Speedy*, and then disappeared. The strangest thing about them was that they had been shown just above the surface of the water, instead of from a masthead, as would usually be the case on a war-ship. The *Speedy* had been slipping quietly along, showing her regular side lights, which, as she was of low freeboard, must also have appeared close to the water from a short distance, and might have been mistaken for a signal. Now she quickly displayed the night-signal of the American blockading fleet, as well as her own private number, but no answer came to either. By the time the *Speedy's* crew were at quarters it was evident, from muffled sounds borne down the wind, that the stranger was a steamer in full retreat.

"Give her a blank shot," ordered Captain Boldwood, and the words had barely left his mouth before the forward six-pounder gun had roared out its summons to halt; but the stranger paid no heed.

A solid shot, well elevated, had as little effect. By this time the despatch-boat was rushing ahead at full speed in the direction the unknown steamer was supposed to have taken. Suddenly her search-light, sweeping the black waters with a broad arc of silver, disclosed a shadowy bulk moving swiftly at right angles to the course they were taking, and heading for a beacon blaze that had sprung up on the starboard or in-shore hand.

"Port your helm!" cried Captain Boldwood. "Mr. Comly, try to disable her. Make every shot tell if possible."

Again and again the six-pounder hurled its messenger of destruction, but apparently without effect.

"Looks as though I couldn't hit the side of a barn at a hundred feet," muttered the Ensign to Ridge, who stood beside him, thrilled by the novel experience. Then he sighted his gun for a third shot, sprang back, and jerked the lanyard. A flash, a roar, a choking cloud of smoke, and then a yell from the *Speedy's* crew. In the glare of the search-light the fugitive steamer was seen to take a sudden sheer, that a minute later was followed by a crash, and then she remained motionless.

Instantly the *Speedy* was slowed down and moved cautiously towards the wreck, with busy lead marking soundings every few seconds. The beacon for which the chase had steered no longer blazed; but in a few minutes the search-light disclosed a wooded shore.

"Have a boat ready, Mr. Comly, and prepare to go on board with half a dozen men."

"Ay, ay, sir."

"May I go with you?" asked Ridge, eagerly.

"Certainly, if the Captain says so."

But, to the young trooper's disappointment, Captain Boldwood refused permission. "Your business is of too important a nature for you to assume any needless risks outside of it," he said.

So Ridge could only watch enviously the departure of the boat with its crew of armed men. It had not been gone two minutes when a bright flame shot from the steamer's deck.

"They have set her on fire and abandoned her!" exclaimed the Captain. "I pray to God, Comly may be cautious. Quartermaster, show the recall."

The words were hardly spoken when there came a great blinding flash, an awful roar, and the *Speedy* listed to her beam ends. A vast pillar of flame leaped a hundred feet into the air, a huge foam-crested wave rolled out to sea, and then all space seemed full of flying fragments. The wreck had been destroyed by an explosion of her own cargo.

"Lower away the yawl! Quick, men! There may be some left to pick up. Yes, Mr. Norris, you may go now."

They rescued Comly, bleeding from a wound in the head, and three of his crew, all more or less injured, but the others had gone down with their boat, crushed beneath a hurtling deck beam.

The *Speedy* stood off and on until daylight enabled her commander to locate the scene of catastrophe and examine what was left of the shattered steamer. He found that she had been run ashore on one of the small outlying cays that are numerous off Cardenas Bay, and with other floating wreckage he picked up a life-preserver on which was painted, "*Manuel Ros*, Barcelona."

"How strangely and unexpectedly things turn out," he said to Ridge as ne turned from examining this telltale relic. "Our Government learned some time ago that the *Manuel Ros* was taking on board at Cadiz a cargo of improved mines, submarine torpedoes, and high explosives for use in Puerto-Rican harbors. It was positively stated that she would not attempt to run the Cuban blockade. Nevertheless, we were all notified to keep a sharp lookout for her, especially around Santiago and Cienfuegos. She was reported to be very fast, and I can well credit it, for there are few ships in these waters can show their heels as she did to the *Speedy*. As it is, I am afraid she would have gained Cardenas Harbor in safety if it had not been for Mr. Comly's last lucky shot, which must have crippled her steering-gear. And to think that a ship which would have been considered a handsome prize by any cruiser should be destroyed by the little *Speedy*. I wonder, though, where the *Wilmington* that generally patrols this vicinity could have been?"

This mystery was explained a little later when the cruiser in question hove in sight, having been lured from her station by a small Spanish gunboat the evening before.

After making his report of what happened, the commander of the *Speedy* again headed his craft to the eastward, and ran all that day, together with most of the following night, within sight of the Cuban coast.

It wanted but an hour of daylight, when Ridge, who was sleeping on deck, was aroused and told that the place of his landing was at hand. A pot of coffee together with a substantial lunch had been prepared for him, and Ensign Comly, whose wound had proved to be slight, was waiting in a boat manned by four sailors.

Señorita was hoisted in a sling and dropped overboard to swim ashore in tow of the boat, and at the very last the *Speedy's* commander whispered the countersign of the Junta that was to open a way through the Cuban lines.

Then the boat was noiselessly shoved off, and slipped away through the chill darkness towards the denser shadow of the land that waited with manifold perils to test the courage of our young trooper.

## CHAPTER XI

### A LIVELY EXPERIENCE OF CUBAN HOSPITALITY

"Good-bye, old man! Good luck, and hope we shall meet again soon."

With these words, accompanied by a warm handclasp, Ensign Dick Comly stepped into his boat, and it was shoved off from the bit of Cuban beach on which Ridge Norris had just been landed. For a couple of minutes the young trooper stood motionless, listening with strained ears to the lessening sound of muffled oars. It was the last link connecting him with home, country, and safety. For a moment he was possessed of such a panic that he was on the point of shouting for Comly to come back and take him away. It did not seem as though he could be left there alone in the dark, and amid all the crowding terrors of that unknown land.

Just then Señorita, who stood dripping and shivering beside him, rubbed her wet nose softly against his cheek, as though begging for sympathy, and in an instant his courage was restored. It was enough that another creature more helpless than he was dependent upon him for guidance and protection.

"It's all right, girl," he whispered, throwing an

arm about the mare's neck. "We'll stick to each other and pull through somehow." Then plucking a handful of dried grass, he gave the animal a brisk rubbing that warmed them both. By the time it was finished, birds were twittering in the dense growth behind them, and the eastern sky was suffused with the glow of coming day.

Knowing nothing of his surroundings, nor what eyes might in a few minutes more discover these new features of the beach, Ridge now removed his slender belongings to a hiding-place behind some bushes, where he also fastened Señorita. Then he set forth to explore the shore with the hope of finding a path into the interior; for to force a way through the tangled chaparral that everywhere approached close to the water's edge seemed hopeless.

He had not gone a dozen paces when Señorita uttered a shrill neigh of distress at being thus deserted, and began a noisy struggle to break loose. With a muttered exclamation of dismay Ridge ran back. It was evident that the mare would not consent to be left.

"Very well," said the young man. "If you can't be reasonable and remain quietly behind for a few minutes, we must make our exploration in company. Perhaps it is better so, after all, for when I do discover a trail we shall be ready to take instant advantage of it, and get the more quickly away from this unpleasantly conspicuous place."

While thus talking in a low tone to the mare,

Ridge was also equipping her for the road. He had just finished tightening the saddle-girth and was about to mount, when Señorita uttered a snort indicative of some strange presence. Turning quickly, her master was confronted by a sight that caused his heart to sink like lead. Only a few paces away stood a young man of dark but handsome features, clad in a well-worn suit of linen and a broad-brimmed palmetto hat. A military belt filled with cartridges encircled his waist, and from it hung an empty scabbard of untanned cowhide, designed to carry a machete. With that weapon held in one hand and a cocked pistol levelled full at Ridge in the other, he presented the appearance of a first-class brigand.

The young trooper made a movement towards his own revolver, but it was instantly checked by the stranger, who said, sternly, in Spanish:

"Hold there! If you but touch a weapon I shall shoot you dead! You are my prisoner, and will obey my commands. That I am prepared to enforce them I will show you."

With this he sounded a low whistle that was answered by a rustle in the bushes, from which half a dozen armed ragamuffins of all shades of swarthiness, from jet black to light chocolate, appeared as though by magic. All were provided with machetes, some carried rifles, and each looked as though it would afford him the greatest pleasure to cut into small pieces the stranger who had invaded their territory.

"You see," said their leader, with a smile, "that you are hopelessly surrounded, and that with a nod I can have you killed."

"Yes, I see," replied Ridge, "and I should be pleased to know into whose hands I have fallen. Are you Cubano or a Spaniard?"

"And I will ask if you are American or Spaniard?"

"But my question came first," insisted Ridge.

"While I am in a position to have mine answered," replied the other, again smiling. "But I will not press it at this moment. We will first seek a place better suited to conversation, since here we are liable to be interrupted. The American gunboats have an unpleasant habit of dropping shells among any party whom they may discover on the beach. Then, too, many Cubanos have been seen about here lately, and they might molest us, while it is also nearly time for the Spanish *lancha* that patrols this coast at sunrise and sunset. So you see— Disarm him!"

This last was an order to two men who had moved noiselessly up behind Ridge while his attention was diverted by their leader. Now they seized our young trooper, took his weapons, and marched him away, though allowing him to retain his hold on Señorita's bridle. For a few paces they crashed through the underbrush, hacking a rude path for the mare with their machetes as they went. Then they struck a dim trail that ended at a grass-grown and little-used road. Crossing this, they entered the grounds of what had evidently been a fine plantation, though a young forest growth was now rapidly spreading over its once well-cultivated fields. A weedy approach between rows of noble trees led to the blackened ruins of a large house and outlying buildings. The stone walls were already overrun with a tangle of vines from which flamed blood-red blossoms. Several horses cropped the rank grass about these ruins, and into one of them, which had been given a temporary thatch of palm leaves, the prisoner was led.

"Here we had begun to break our fast when your mare notified us of your proximity," said the leader, who had already motioned to his men to loose their hold on the young American. "Now if you will honor us with your company, we will resume that interrupted pleasure. Manuel, we wait to be served."

Upon this a grinning negro brought in a basketful of yams that had evidently been roasted among the ashes of an open fire, and set it on a rude table. Beside it he placed a calabash containing a drink mixed of water, lime-juice, and brown sugar. "Let us eat," said the host, reaching for one of the ash-encoated yams. "But hold," he added, as though with a sudden thought. "Excuse me for a moment." Thus saying, he stepped outside, only to return with Ridge's saddle-bags, which he coolly opened. "Coffee, as I live!" he cried, "and hard biscuit, the first bread I have seen in many a month! Señor, we are under obligations to you for these welcome additions to our *menu*. Manuel, hast thou forgotten how to make coffee, strong, and black as thine own ebony face? Waste thou not one precious grain, or, by holy St. Jago, I will blow out thy meagre brains."

Provoked as Ridge was at seeing his entire stock of provisions thus appropriated to be expended on a single meal, he was not in a position to remonstrate. So, a little later, when a revised edition of breakfast was pronounced ready, he sat down with the host whom he did not yet know whether to consider as friend or foe, and ate heartily of the food thus provided.

The furnishing of that rude table was unique, for, mingled with shells from the beach and those of cocoanuts, both of which were used in place of cups, gourds, plantain-leaves, and wooden trays, appeared several dishes of cut glass and dainty china, generally cracked or chipped, and looking wofully out of place.

Seeing that Ridge noticed these, the host said, carelessly:

"Ah yes, señor, we have seen better days!" Then, lighting a cigarette, he continued, more sternly, "Now, sir, can you give any reason why I should not have you led out and shot as a spy?"

"You would not dare do such a thing!" replied Ridge, indignantly.

"Oh! wouldn't I? My friend, you do not realize into whose hands you have fallen. Now, merely to prove that I have both the inclination and power to carry out my threat, I will have you shot. Lope! Garzo!"

Two of the ragged bandits immediately appeared.

"Bind me the arms of this man and blindfold him."

The order was deftly obeyed.

"Now take him from my sight and shoot him."

Seizing Ridge by the shoulders, the men began to drag him away.

Until this moment he had not known whether to acknowledge himself an American or claim to be a Spaniard, nor had he believed that the extremely courteous leader of bandits with whom he had just breakfasted, and who might be either a Cuban patriot or a Spanish guerilla, would do him serious injury. Now, moved by an agony of terror, he shouted out the word whispered to him a few hours before by the commander of the *Speedy*, the secret countersign of the Cuban Junta.

Its effect was magical. The men who were dragging him to a summary execution loosed their hold and stared at him in amazement, while the young leader sprang to where Ridge stood, tore the bandages from his eyes, severed his bonds, and embraced him.

"Why, my brother, did you not disclose your identity long ago?" he said.

"Because," replied Ridge, in a voice that still trembled from his recent fright, "I knew not to which side you belonged."

"What! Did you for a moment think that I

might be a vile Spaniard? I, Enrico del Concha, a Cuban of the Cubans? Alas! that such a suspicion should fall upon one of my name."

"And what," inquired Ridge, "did you take me for?"

"A Spanish spy, of course. Do you not speak the language without even a Cuban accent? Did you not decline to tell me how or what you were? Above all, did you not carry on your person despatches addressed to certain Spanish generals?"

Ridge clapped a hand to his breast pocket.

"Yes, señor, they are gone," laughed the other. "My rogues are clever thieves, and took them from you when we first met, together with your money, for which they were searching. Hereafter you must provide for your private papers a place of greater safety. Now let us have one more cup of that delicious coffee while you confide to me who you are and why you are here."

## CHAPTER XII

### DENOUNCED BY A FRIEND

UNDER the circumstances, Ridge felt that a frank avowal of his personality and present plans would be wiser than any attempt at deception, and this he proceeded to make. To all that he had to tell the bandit leader paid closest attention, and listened without a word of interruption until the narrative was finished. Then he said:

"It is indeed great news that the Americans are about to invade Cuba. Until now they have promised much and done worse than nothing, since, by their blockade of Cuban ports, they have only starved to death thousands of miserable reconcentrados. Now if they will proceed with judgment and are not swept off by fevers, something may be accomplished. At the same time, from the ignorance displayed in sending on so important a mission as yours one so ill equipped for it, I cannot hope for much from them."

Ridge flushed hotly. "What do you mean?" he asked.

"I mean," replied the other, coolly rolling a cigarette as he spoke, "that you have shown yourself to be about as fit for the duty you have undertaken as a babe in arms. Did you not, upon landing, waste a whole hour of precious darkness during which you might have gained a safe distance from the always-guarded coast? Did you not allow yourself to be betrayed by your horse, and captured without resistance? Did you not lose your despatches at the outset, and almost your life as well? Are you not at this moment densely ignorant of the route you are to travel, and of how to meet the enemies you will encounter on every hand?

"Yes, my friend, brave and resolute as you may be, you are also but a babe in your undertaking. Your only forethought lay in securing the countersign of the Junta, which has for the moment saved your life, since I should certainly have caused you to be shot but for it. Also, if I had not discovered you, the Spanish hawks who patrol the coast would have had you in their clutches a few minutes later. Nor do you at this moment know how to find your way to Holguin, much less to Santiago."

"But," argued Ridge, whose self-conceit and confidence in his own ability to carry out the mission he had so bravely undertaken were rapidly oozing away, "I have a good map of the country, a good horse, plenty of money with which to hire guides, am well armed, and could make a good fight if necessary. I speak Spanish perfectly, am dark of complexion, possess the countersign of the Junta for Cubans, and letters from the chief of the Spanish secret service for Spaniards. Why, then, may I not succeed as well as another?"

"You *had* those things; but, with the exception of your ability to speak Spanish, your darkness of skin, and the countersign, all of them have been taken from you."

"But you will restore them?"

"And if I should, would they serve you? Do you imagine that any true Cuban would disclose to an utter stranger the military secrets of his country for money? If you do, you are sadly mistaken. Could you fight an enemy who would lie in ambush and shoot you in the back, reserving the examination of your despatches until you were dead? Even should you succeed in presenting those same despatches to a Spanish general, do you not know that he would hold you prisoner, or at least delay your departure until he had transmitted them to Havana for verification? Yet you hope to gain a complete knowledge of the military situation in this great province, and rejoin your friends more than a hundred miles away within a week. Amigo, you are very ignorant."

"Possibly I am," admitted Ridge, "but I have learned much from you within a short time; and if you will let me go, I will still undertake to accomplish my task within the time allotted to me."

"I admire your spirit," replied del Concha, "and will gladly release you, with all your property restored; but before so doing I wish to make some suggestions. In the first place, your people should have chosen an intelligent Cuban for this work—a man like myself, for instance."

Ridge was on the point of saying that his superior officers had feared to trust a Cuban, but prudently refrained from so doing.

"As they did not have the sense for that," continued the speaker, "it is most fortunate that you have met me, for I can give you, in a few words, the position and strength of every Spanish force in the province, as well as the location and condition of the Cuban armies, to which I will also gladly forward news of the anticipated American landing. Thus you will be free to make your way, directed by guides whom I will furnish, straight to Santiago without encountering any dangers other than those incident to travel through a rough country."

"While thanking you for your kind offer," replied Ridge, "I must still decline it. My orders are to communicate directly with the Spanish commanders at Holguin and Jiguani, and I shall certainly attempt to carry them out, since the first lesson taught every American soldier is that of absolute and unquestioning obedience to orders."

"My dear Lieutenant!" exclaimed del Concha—for this was the rank that Ridge had seen fit to assume—"I begin to perceive why you were chosen for this hopeless task, and though I utterly disapprove your proposed course of action, I cannot but admire your resolution. Also I cannot find it in my heart to leave you to your own helpless devices. Therefore I shall accompany you to the vicinity of

Holguin. Then I shall at least be on hand to learn your fate as soon as it is decided."

Willing as he would have been to set forth alone, Ridge was glad to have the company of one so familiar with the country as del Concha appeared, and one also whom he believed he might trust. His confidence in the acquaintance thus strangely made was strengthened a little later as they rode together, and the latter, in answer to his questions, disclosed a portion of his own history.

"I came to this place last evening," he said, "in the hope of getting a few shots at the Spanish *lancha*, which, as I told you, patrols the coast twice daily; for Spaniards have become so scarce of late, and confine themselves so closely to the larger towns, that it is sometimes difficult to maintain my record of one for each day."

"What do you mean?" asked Ridge.

"I mean that during the past year I have personally killed, or caused to be killed, a Spanish soldier for each day that has passed."

The young American regarded his companion with horror.

"Moreover," continued the other, coolly, "I have sworn to maintain that average so long as I live and the present war continues. When I found you this morning I thought my duty for the day was accomplished, but now it is with pleasure that I shall look elsewhere for my dead Spaniard of this date."

"Are all Cubans animated by your spirit?" asked

Ridge, whose soul revolted at this calm discussion of what seemed to him cold-blooded murder.

"All who have suffered what I have are, or should be, filled with my longing for vengeance," answered del Concha. "Listen. The ruined plantation we have just left was my home. There I was born. There in the care of a loving father and a devoted mother, in company with a brother who was older than I, and a younger sister, I grew up. In spite of cruel taxation, we were wealthy; in spite of unrighteous laws, we were happy. Finally Spain's oppression of Cuba became unbearable, and the war to throw it off was begun. My father refused to take part in the rebellion, but my brother joined the insurgents and was killed in battle. I took his place; and, because his sons aided the insurrection, my noble father, still loyal to Spain, was seized by the Spaniards and thrown into prison. Two days later, without trial or previous warning, he was shot to death in the prison-yard.

"For giving bread to starving women and children whose husbands and fathers fought in the Cuban army, my mother and sister were driven from their home to the nearest city, where the former, always delicate, died, literally of starvation, and from which my sister disappeared, so that I do not know her fate. At that time, also, our house was stripped by the soldiers of everything that could be carried away, and then burned. It is for this record of crime that I determined to spare no Spaniard who should come within my reach."

"I am afraid," said Ridge, slowly, with a clear vision of his own dear home and its loved inmates in his mind, "that in your place I should act as you have acted."

Although the city of Holguin lies only about twenty miles from the place where Ridge landed on the coast, the way to it was so obstructed, first by swamps and dense forests, and later by wooded hills and swollen streams, that evening shadows were closing in when Ridge and his ragged escort came within sight of its low roofs. On the still air were borne to their ears at the same moment the clear notes of Spanish bugles sounding the "Retreat."

Ridge had speculated much that day concerning his reception by the Spaniards, and as to how he should enter their lines. Now del Concha proposed a plan that seemed feasible.

"Ride in at full speed," he said, "while I with my men will follow as though in hot pursuit close up to the lines. Of course we will exchange shots, though both must carefully fire too high to do any damage. Is it well? Then adios, my friend, until we meet again."

A few minutes later the newly posted Spanish guard was startled by the sound of shots, and then by the sight of a fugitive horseman speeding towards them, followed closely by a party of mounted insurgents who were firing at him. Drums were beat and trumpets sounded. A small body of troops hastily advanced from the city, opening their ranks to receive the panting horse and its apparently exhausted rider, but closing them to give an ineffective volley against his pursuers, who were now flying in consternation.

Half an hour afterwards, Ridge, addressed as Señor Remelios, stood in the presence of General Pando, the Spanish commander of the eastern diocese of the island, and second only to the Captain-General, who was carefully reading a despatch just handed him by the young trooper.

"You say, señor, that you have just come from Gibara, where you were secretly landed last night?"

"Yes, General."

"Also from this note, signed by Lieutenant Carranza, I learn that the Americans are about to land in force at Cienfuegos."

"Such are Señor Carranza's latest advices."

"Um! They conflict, however, with news just brought from the south that a landing has already been effected at Guantanamo."

Here the old soldier peered keenly at our hero, who experienced a thrill of uneasiness.

At this moment there came a challenge from the sentry stationed at the door. It was satisfactorily answered, and another individual hurriedly entered the room.

"Your Excellency," said this person, making a profound salute, " pardon my intrusion; but I am come to denounce the man now standing before you as a Yankee spy. His despatch is a forgery and utterly false, since the American army is not to land at Cienfuegos, but at Santiago."

Just here Ridge obtained his first view of the speaker's face, and was overwhelmed with dismay to recognize in it the features of the man who had ridden with him all that day under the guise of a Cuban patriot. It was that of Enrico del Concha.

## CHAPTER XIII

### TO BE SHOT AT SUNRISE

NEVER in his life had our hero experienced a feeling of such utter helplessness as he did upon recognizing del Concha. The treachery unfolded by the man's words was beyond his comprehension, and he knew not how to combat it. For a moment he stared speechless at the traitor, then he turned to the General, who was gazing at him with stern inquiry.

"Your Excellency," said Ridge, "the man who thus seeks to gain your favor, and, as I suppose, a reward, by denouncing me, is doubly a traitor. He kills Spaniards at every opportunity, and now seeks my life at your hands because he knows that I am one. It is true that I was captured by him and his band of Cuban ruffians. To save my life, I told him the story that he now brings to you. After thus allaying his suspicions, I seized a favorable opportunity to escape. By the superior swiftness of my horse I finally reached this place in safety, though pursued by him to your very lines and hotly fired upon, as can be proved by many witnesses. Now, therefore, I, José Remelios, bearer of despatches from the Señor Carranza, denounce this man as a doubly dyed traitor, and demand that he be arrested on a charge of being a Cuban spy."

"Have you ever seen him kill a Spaniard?" asked General Pando.

Ridge was obliged to admit that he had not.

"Then how do you know that he has done so?"

"From his own boastful confession. He claims to have taken the life of a Spanish soldier for every day of the last year."

The General smiled. "That is certainly a very boastful claim," he said, "but one not to be believed for a moment. Think you, sir, that such a number of Spaniards could be killed without my knowledge? or that, in any case, one man could thus overcome the brave, experienced, and well-armed soldiers of Spain? Your credulity, señor, is refreshing. Also I have no hesitation in telling you that ever since I took command of the eastern diocese, this man, recommended to me by my predecessor in office, has been the most faithful and valuable of my secret agents among the Cubans. Time and again he has furnished early information of important events which has subsequently proved correct in every detail. With such a record in his favor, am I now to doubt him upon the mere word of a stranger? No, señor, the honor of a Spaniard forbids. I am obliged, therefore—"

Just here came an interruption of voices at the door. Hearing them, del Concha, who had remained silent during the foregoing conversation and apparently careless of what was said concerning him, uttered a few hurried words to the General in a low tone, and disappeared behind a screen that stood close at hand. Directly afterwards a lieutenant and two soldiers entered with a prisoner, whom Ridge recognized as one of the ragged Cubans who had escorted him to Holguin.

"General," said the officer, saluting, "I bring a Cuban deserter who claims to have information of pressing importance that he will impart to no one but yourself, so I have ventured to intrude; but if it is your pleasure, I will remove him and seek to extort his secret."

"Oh no," replied the commander; "it is not worth the trouble. Let him speak, and quickly, for I am pressed with business."

"I come, Excellenza," began the deserter, in a trembling voice, "with the hope of clemency and a reward, to notify your Excellency that this señor"— here he pointed to Ridge—"is not what he pretends. I was of a band who captured him on the coast, and I overheard his confession to our leader. From his own mouth, therefore, I learned that he is a spy, and—"

"An American bearing false despatches," interrupted the General, irritably. "You see I already know all that you would say. Remove your prisoner, soldados." Then, in a lower tone to the officer, he added: "Take him away and dispose of him. Such *canaille* are as troublesome as fleas. Immediately upon completing the job you may return, as I have other business for you."

With a salute, the officer hurried after his men. At the same time del Concha emerged from his place of concealment, and the General, turning to Ridge, said :

"You have doubtless noted, señor, how quickly the information concerning yourself brought by this gentleman is confirmed. Therefore you will not be surprised to have me order you into confinement until your case can be reported to Havana"—at this moment came the startling sound of a volley of musketry, evidently fired close at hand—"and a decision concerning it received from the Captain-General," concluded the speaker, paying no heed to the firing.

As Ridge was about to utter a protest, the officer who had left the room a minute before, re-entered it, saluted with stiff precision, and stood awaiting orders.

"Lieutenant Navarro," said the General, "you will remove this gentleman, who is charged with being an American spy, and bid the officer in charge of the guard-house hold him in closest custody until he receives further instructions. Adios, Señor Remelios. May your night's rest be peaceful."

Perceiving that resistance or protest would be useless, Ridge passively allowed himself to be led away. A file of soldiers stood outside, and, surrounded by these, he was marched to the guard-house, where, after being searched and relieved of everything contained by his pockets, he was led into a bare, cell-like room.

A wooden stool and a heap of filthy straw in one corner constituted its sole furnishing. Through a grating in the door came the flickering light of a lamp burning in the corridor, while outer air was admitted by a small iron-barred opening in one of the side walls some six feet above the floor. The place reeked with dampness, and, in spite of these openings, its air was foul and stifling. A few minutes after Ridge entered it, and as he sat in dumb despair, vainly striving to realize his unhappy situation, a soldier brought him a bowl of bean porridge and a jug of water. Without a word, he set these down and departed.

A little later other soldiers came and gazed curiously at him through the grated door, always speaking of him as "el Yanko," and making merry at his expense. Thus several hours passed, and he still sat motionless, trying to think; but his brain was in a whirl, and he seemed as powerless to concentrate his thoughts as he was friendless. He realized dimly that at regular intervals a guard, pacing the outer corridor, paused before the door of his cell to peer in at him, and so make sure of his presence; but he paid slight attention to this official scrutiny.

Suddenly his ear caught a sound strange to that place—a girlish voice laughing merrily and evidently exchanging brisk repartee with the soldiers in the guard-room. It was a pleasanter sound than any he had heard, and he listened to it eagerly. After a little the voice seemed to draw nearer, and he could distinguish the words, "el Yanko." He, then, was the subject of that gay conversation. A moment later, from the same source, came an expression that numbed him with the awfulness of its possible meaning. "To be shot at sunrise? Poor fellow!" Could he be the "poor fellow" meant? Of course not; but then he might be. Such a summary disposition of prisoners was not unknown to Spanish jailers.

While his mind was busy with this startling question the laughing voice, now lowered almost to a whisper, approached his door, and he became conscious of a scrutiny through the grating. Also a discussion was going on outside, and he heard:

"No, no, not a smile, not a word, unless you open the door so that I may see el Yanko. I have never seen one in all my life—never."

A short pause, then a key turned, and the door was gently opened. Two figures entered. A soldier and a slender girl, who clung fearfully to his arm. They stood and looked at Ridge as he sat on his wooden stool, and he stared back. For a moment the three gazed at one another in silence. Then the girl exclaimed, pettishly:

"If that is all your famous Yanko amounts to, I have already seen enough, since he looks exactly like other men, only more ugly than some. Come, let us go."

With this she playfully turned her companion

about and pushed him from the cell. As she did so she made a quick backward movement with her right hand, and something fell on the straw pallet as though flung there. A second later the door was relocked, and, with merry laughter again echoing through the dim corridor, they were gone.

Curiously Ridge fumbled in the musty bedding until he found a small packet enveloped in brown paper. He opened it eagerly. Inside were two tiny steel saws, made from a watch spring, and a little tube of oil. There was also a bit of white paper on which was writing. By holding this close to the lamp-lighted grating, Ridge read:

"You have only till daylight. Saw out a bar and squeeze through. Friends will await you outside. Destroy this." There was no signature.

"What friends can I have in this place?" thought the young trooper, as he nervously chewed the bit of paper to a pulp. At the same time he was tremulous with a new hope. "Perhaps I can do it," he said, "and anything will be better than sitting in idleness, with a prospect of being shot at sunrise."

Standing on his wooden stool he could easily reach the lower end of the iron bars closing the cell window, and he at once began work on them. At first he seemed to produce about as much effect as would the gnawing of a mouse, but after a while his tiny saw was buried in the tough iron. Then footsteps approached, and Ridge had barely time to fling himself on the vile-smelling pallet before a sentry was peering in at the grating. A ray of light fell where he lay, but fortunately failed to reach the side on which the barred aperture was located. So the prisoner made a long bunch of the straw, covered it with his coat, and placed his water-jug at one end, thus causing the whole to bear a rude resemblance to a human figure.

After that he worked steadily, only pausing at the sound of footsteps, but not leaving the scene of his operations. He found that he must cut two bars instead of only one, and a saw snapped in twain when the first was but half severed. After that he handled the other with intense caution, and his heart throbbed painfully with anxiety as the work neared completion.

For hours he toiled, and he knew that daylight could not be far off when the second bar was finally cut. To bend it aside took all his strength, and so occupied was he in doing this that for the first time that night he heeded not a sound of footsteps in the corridor.

"What goes on here?" questioned a harsh voice, and Ridge's heart leaped into his mouth. With desperate energy he wrenched the bars to one side, hearing as he did so a fumbling at the lock of his door. Utilizing his strength to the utmost, he pulled himself up, forced his body through the narrow opening, and pitched headlong to the ground outside. At the same time came fierce shouts, a pistol-shot, and a great clamor from the place he had left.

But strong hands were helping him to his feet,

and a voice was saying in his ears: "You have done well, amigo. Now we must fly for our lives."

Of course it could not be; but to Ridge's senses, confused by the shock of his fall, it seemed as though the voice was that of the false friend who had betrayed him

## CHAPTER XIV

### REFUGEES IN THE MOUNTAINS

WITHOUT a knowledge of direction or purpose, Ridge suffered himself to be guided by his unknown friend through several narrow streets. They ran at top speed and in silence, but behind them came a clamor of soldiers from the guard-house. By their shouts that a prisoner was escaping, these aroused that portion of the town, and frightened occupants of squalid houses caught shadowy glimpses of the fugitives as they sped past. To the pursuers these same spectators pointed eagerly the course taken by those who fled, so that the scent of the chase was kept hot.

A sudden turn disclosed three horses, one bearing a rider, and all standing motionless. A glad whinny of recognition came from one as Ridge Norris gained its side, and in another moment his own Señorita was speeding him away from the scene of his recent danger.

As the three swept through the outer picket-line unharmed by its thick flying bullets, they were startled by a clatter of hoofs at right angles to their course, and coming swiftly towards them. A cavalry patrol warned by the uproar, and catching sight of the fugitives in the growing dawn, was striving to intercept them. They also fired as they rode, and two of those who fled bent low over their horses' necks that they might offer as small a mark as possible. Not so the young American, who now found himself under fire for the first time in his life. He had found his rifle still attached to the saddle; and now, with every drop of blood in his body at fighting heat, he sat erect, half turned, and fired back until every shot in his magazine was exhausted. As a result, several of the pursuers dropped from the chase; but it was hotly maintained by the others, who also kept up a desultory shooting.

They had gained a good mile from town when suddenly one of Ridge's companions uttered a sharp cry, in a voice distinctly feminine, and reeled in her saddle. The other, whom Ridge now knew to be del Concha, leaped from his horse and caught her in his arms as she fell.

"We must make a stand and fight!" he cried, as Ridge reined Señorita to a sudden halt beside him. "Drive the beasts ahead and conceal yourself on the other side. I will remain here."

They were already among the foothills of the Almiqui Mountains, and had just passed a low crest which, for the moment, hid them from their pursuers. The ambush was so quickly arranged that, two minutes later when these appeared, they saw nothing of it and heard only a rush of horses' hoofs in the ravine below.

With a yell the Spanish cavalrymen put spurs to their steeds and dashed down the declivity. The first two were allowed to pass. Then came a double flash of flame from the bushes and one of the riders fell, while another uttered the cry of a wounded man. Two more were killed before the panic-stricken horsemen were borne beyond range. Those who remained unhurt left the road and fled for their lives down the bed of a little stream that crossed it at the foot of the hill. The wounded man was despatched by del Concha where he lay, before Ridge could interpose a word in his behalf.

"And why not?" asked the Cuban, as he coolly wiped his machete on the grass. "Can the blood-debt that I owe them ever be paid? Are they not adding to it every day? Even now, does not she who is dearest of all the world to me lie wounded at their hands?"

"But I thought you were in their service, and that they trusted you."

"So they do trust me, and to their sorrow," replied del Concha, with a bitter laugh. "But there is no time for explanations. A precious life hangs in the balance, and only instant action may save it. If you can recover the horses, or even one of them, all may go well. If not, there is little room for hope."

Without reply Ridge whistled a shrill note that echoed sharply among the hills. The distant neigh of a horse came in answer, and he started on a run down the road. At the foot of the slope he encountered Señorita coming back to meet him; and springing to her back he went in pursuit of her companions whom he soon discovered grazing by the wayside. At sight of him they fled at full speed; but they might as well have raced with the wind as with the fleet-footed mare; and, within ten minutes from the time of leaving del Concha, Ridge returned, leading the horse the Cuban had ridden. The other was left, tied to a tree where he had captured it.

Del Concha was holding in his arms their wounded comrade, apparently a slender youth, whose face was now disclosed to Ridge for the first time by the light of the newly risen sun. Although it was of deathly pallor, and the eyes were closed, he instantly recognized it as belonging to the girl of the laughing voice who had so cleverly contrived to aid him the evening before.

"Yes," said del Concha, noting the look of recognition, "it was she who carried you the saws and message. She is the bravest girl in all Cuba, and the sweetest. It was for my sake and that of her country that she aided you; for she is a devoted patriot, and my *fiancée*. We were to be married as soon as an American army landed. She would have it so. Now if she dies, I cannot bear it."

While he spoke, the grief-stricken man, in whom there was slight resemblance to the debonair bandit of the day before, laid his burden gently down, and mounted the horse that Ridge had recovered.

"Now give her to me," he said; and, tenderly lifting the light form, Ridge placed it once more in his arms. The girl had been shot in the back, and the cruel Mauser bullet, long but slender as a lead-pencil, had passed through her body.

"My only hope is to get her to the nearest camp of refugees, and that is still five miles away," said del Concha.

After that they rode in silence, the sorrowing lover, with his precious burden leading the way, and the young American oppressed by the sadness of the incident for which he felt wholly, though unwittingly to blame, following with the spare horse. Mingled with our hero's self-reproach was also a decided curiosity as to how del Concha would explain the double part he had played the evening before.

As they advanced into the heart of the mountains, ever climbing, their road grew rougher and narrower, until finally it was a mere trail. Although they passed occasional ruins of huts, they did not see one that was inhabited or habitable. Neither did they encounter a human being until their destination was reached, though for the last mile of their progress they were constantly watched by wild-looking figures that peered at them from behind rocks or bushes. Often, after a single glance at the horsemen, these ragged scouts would dart away, scurrying through the brush with the noiseless speed of rabbits, and one able to see them would have observed that all took the same direction. It was towards a camp of Cuban refugees, snugly hidden in one of the most inaccessible recesses of the mountains, and to it they bore the news of approaching visitors.

Therefore the camp was in a state of expectancy even before the new-comers were challenged by its outpost, and as del Concha had long since been recognized, they received a cordial greeting. The wounded girl was at once taken to a commodious hut, where she could be cared for by nurses of her own sex, while a substantial breakfast, roughly cooked and of the simplest character, was made ready for the two men. It was served on the ground just outside the hut of the Cuban General commanding the camp and its few hundreds of ragged soldiers. This officer expressed great joy upon learning from Ridge that an American army was about to land in Cuba, and promised to harass any expedition sent against it from Holguin.

After breakfast, while del Concha was gone to inquire concerning his sweetheart, the General took Ridge to his private observatory, a superb palm, occupying an eminence, and towering above the surrounding forest. From its leafy crown one could look directly down on Holguin and, with a good glass, clearly discern the movements of its garrison.

While thus alone with the General our young trooper asked questions about del Concha.

"He is one of the bravest and most patriotic of Cubans," declared the other, warmly. "No one has done more than he to advance our cause."

"Has he ever been suspected of being a Spanish spy?" asked Ridge.

"Certainly not, señor. Such a question is almost an insult."

"Yet the lieutenant has good cause for his inquiry," said del Concha himself, who joined them at that moment. "Moreover, he is entitled to an explanation from me, which I will hasten to give before he shall demand it."

"It will afford me great pleasure to hear it," said Ridge, "for some of your recent actions have been, to say the least, very puzzling."

"As, for instance, when I denounced you to General Pando. Certainly you must have thought badly of me at that time. I did it, however, to save both you and myself, since shortly after you left us I learned that one of my troop had deserted for the purpose of betraying you to the Spanish General, who, he hoped and believed, would give him a liberal reward for so doing. As Pando supposes me to be one of his agents—in which capacity, by-the-way, I have been able to render valuable service to Cuba—"

"Indeed, yes," muttered the General.

"—I saw at once," continued del Concha, "that in order to save us both I must forestall the deserter and do the denouncing myself. You witnessed the result in the reception accorded the man when he appeared with his stale news, and are aware of his fate."

"No, I am not," said Ridge.

"Did you not hear the volley by which he was shot within one minute after being led from Pando's presence?"

"Was that it?" asked the young American, in an awe-stricken tone.

"Certainly; and served him exactly right, too. Also saved me the job of punishing him. After that, and after you had been removed, Pando confided to me that, as yours was a perfectly clear case, he should not bother Blanco with it, but should promptly dispose of it by having you shot at sunrise. He also honored me with a mission to Santiago, on which he desired that I should set forth immediately. I of course accepted, only with a mental resolve to take you along, and this, with Eva's help, I was in a fair way to accomplish when the dear girl received her terrible wound."

"Bless her!" exclaimed Ridge, fervently, now fully realizing for the first time all that had been done for him. "I hope, with all my heart, that her wound is not serious."

"I fear it is, though for the present she seems quite comfortable."

"And you are going to Santiago?"

"Not one step beyond this point until she is out of danger."

"But I must go," said Ridge, decidedly.

"Certainly; and I have a competent guide ready to start at any moment, and conduct you on the next stage of your journey."

## CHAPTER XV

#### DIONYSIO CAPTURES A SPANIARD

WHILE Ridge was greatly disappointed at losing the guidance and companionship of the young Cuban, in whom his confidence was now wholly restored, he could not, under the circumstances, urge him to go farther, nor did he dare longer delay his own journey. With Señorita, all his belongings, including his undelivered despatches, and the money stolen when he was captured by del Concha, had been restored to him. So he now added to his outfit a grass-woven hammock that he purchased in the refugee camp, and was then ready to set forth.

The new guide awaiting him was a coal-black negro named Dionysio, who was of such huge stature that the other Cubans seemed pygmies beside him. He was armed only with a great machete, ground to exceeding sharpness, and he disdained to ride a horse, declaring that he could, on foot, cover a greater distance in less time than any horse on the island, which Ridge was able to credit after a short experience with his ebony guide. Besides, being a big man and a very strong one, Dionysio was a silent man, as taciturn as an Indian, and never spoke except upon necessity.

When Ridge was introduced to him he was sitting in the shade of a corojo-palm, smoking a cigarette and lovingly fingering the razor-like edge of his machete.

"This is the Señor Americano whom you are to guide to Jiguani, and afterwards, if he requires it, to Santiago," said del Concha.

Dionysio looked keenly at Ridge, but uttered no word.

"He is ready to start."

The negro stood up, to signify that he was also ready.

"You will not let the Spaniards kill him." Dionysio tapped his machete significantly.

"Well, my friend, adios," said del Concha, "and may you come safely to your journey's end!"

Accepting this farewell as a signal to move, the black giant set forth at a swinging pace, and, in order not to lose sight of him, Ridge was obliged instantly to follow. In another minute, therefore, they had crossed the clearing, plunged again into the forest, and the refugee camp was as lost to their view as though it had not existed.

The silent guide bore on his shoulders a burden of yams rolled in a hammock, but it in no way interfered with the freedom of his movements. For miles he maintained, up hill and down, the same speed with which he had set out, and which so taxed Señorita's endurance that Ridge was finally forced to call a halt. The heat of the sun was by this time intense, while the forest steamed from a succession of brief but drenching showers that had swept over it since they started.

As Dionysio comprehended what was wanted he proceeded, without a word, to construct a small bower of branches and palm leaves, beneath which he slung Ridge's hammock. The young trooper's eyes were so leaden with sleep that he had no sooner slipped into this than he was lost in a dreamless slumber.

When he next awoke, greatly refreshed by his long nap, the great heat of the day was past, and the shadows of coming evening produced a pleasant coolness. For a few minutes Ridge lay in a state of lazy content, gazing with languid interest at his surroundings. The sky, so far as he could see it, was cloudless, the crisp leaves of a tall palm close at hand rustled in a light breeze like the patter of rain, gayly plumaged paroquets and nonpareils flitted across his line of vision, and the air was filled with the pleasant odor of burning wood, mingled with the fragrance of a cigarette that Dionysio smoked while squatted on his heels before a small fire. A little beyond, Señorita, tethered to a tree, cropped at a small patch of coarse grass, and—but Ridge could not credit his senses until he had rubbed his eyes vigorously to make sure that they were doing their duty—another horse was sharing the grass-plot with her. As he assured himself of this, Ridge sat up, and was about to demand an explanation of the negro, when his question was checked by another sight still more amazing.

A human figure staring fixedly at him with glaring eyes was rigidly bound to the trunk of a nearby tree. It was that of a young man in the uniform of a Spanish officer. His face was covered with blood, upon which a swarm of flies had settled, and he was so securely fastened that he could not move hand nor foot. He was also gagged so that he could make no sound beyond an inarticulate groan, which he uttered when he saw that Ridge was awake and looking at him.

With an exclamation of dismay the young American leaped from his hammock. At the same moment Dionysio rose to his feet with a broad grin on his black face, and spoke for the first time since Ridge had made his acquaintance.

"Him Holguin Spaniard," he said, pointing to the prisoner. "Me catch him. Keep him for Americano to kill. Now you shoot him."

Thus saying, the negro handed Ridge a loaded pistol that he had taken from the Spaniard, and then stepped aside with an air of ferocious expectancy to note with what skill the latter would fire at the human target thus provided.

Mechanically Ridge accepted the weapon, and with blazing eyes strode towards the hapless Spaniard, who uttered a groan of agony, evidently believing that his last moment had arrived. As the young trooper passed the place where Dionysio had squatted, he snatched the negro's big machete from the ground.

"'HIM HOLAGUN SPANIARD. NOW YOU SHOOT HIM,' SAID THE CUBAN"

At this the latter chuckled with delight, evidently believing that the blood-thirsty Americano was about to hew his victim in pieces, an operation that, to him, would be vastly more entertaining than a mere shooting. Then he stared in bewilderment; for, instead of cutting the prisoner down, Ridge began to sever the lashings by which he was bound. As the keen-edged machete cut through the last of these, the released man fell forward in a faint, and the young American, catching him in his arms, laid him on the sward. "Bring water!" he ordered, with a sharp tone of authority, and the negro obeyed.

"You no kill him?" he asked, as he watched Ridge bathe the blood from the unconscious man's face.

"Not now," was the evasive answer. "Where did you get him?"

Little by little, one word at a time, he gained from the taciturn negro an idea of what had taken place while he slept. It seemed that, while he had followed rough mountain trails in his roundabout course to and from the refugee camp, there was a much better road to which they had closely approached, when he was forced by exhaustion to call a halt. After he fell asleep, Dionysio, going for water to a spring that he knew of, had detected a sound of hoof-beats advancing along this road from the direction of Holguin. Concealing himself near the spring, he waited until the horseman, a Spanish officer, rode up to it. Then he leaped upon the man, dragged him to the ground, and had him secured almost before the astonished officer knew what was happening. He was also dazed by a wound in the head received as he was hurled from his horse.

Dionysio was on the point of killing him, as he had many a Spaniard, but reflecting that the Americano whom he was guiding would doubtless enjoy that pleasure, he generously decided to yield it to him and reserve the victim until Ridge should finish his nap. So, after gagging the Spaniard, that he might not disturb him who slept, Dionysio flung him across his shoulder and carried him to camp. There he secured him to a tree so that Ridge might see him upon awakening, and then calmly resumed his duties as camp cook and sentry. The unfortunate prisoner, wounded, bound, and powerless to move or speak, tormented by heat and insects, and parched by a burning thirst, had thus suffered for hours, while the young American who was to kill him slept close at hand, blissfully unaware of his presence.

As Ridge pityingly cleansed the face of this enemy whose present sufferings had been terminated by unconsciousness, he all at once recognized it as that of the officer who had conveyed him from General Pando's quarters to the guard-house in Holguin. At the same time, noting a slight rustle of paper somewhere in the man's clothing, he began a search for it, and finally discovered a despatch in an official envelope. Carefully opening this without breaking the seal, he found it to contain two papers. One was a personal note from General Pando to the Spanish commander at Jiguani, calling his attention to the other, which was an order to set forth at once with his entire force for Santiago, where an American army was about to land, and where he would be joined by 5000 troops from Holguin.

"This is interesting," commented Ridge, "and of course must not be allowed to reach its destination. So I will just put in its place my Carranza despatch to this same gentleman, informing him that the Americans are to land at Cienfuegos. It will have added weight if it appears to come from General Pando, and will surely start him off in a direction where he can do no harm.

"I wonder, though, what I had best do with you," he continued, meditatively, addressing the unconscious form beside him. "Of course you will recognize me as soon as you are able to sit up and take notice. Of course, also, I can't kill you in cold blood; nor can I turn you over to the tender mercies of Dionysio, for that would amount to exactly the same thing. I don't dare let you go, and I can't be bothered with you as a prisoner; so what on earth I am to do with you I'm sure I don't know. I almost wish you wouldn't wake up at all."

Just here, owing to Ridge's kindly ministrations, the cause of his perplexity opened his eyes, looked the young American full in the face, and smiled a faint smile in which recognition and gratitude were equally blended.

## CHAPTER XVI

### ASLEEP WHILE ON GUARD

OF course there was no further thought of continuing the journey that evening, for the Spanish officer was in no condition to travel, and our young trooper was not one to desert even an enemy who was helpless and in distress. So he informed Dionysio that they would remain where they were until morning, and ordered him to make things as comfortable as possible for the night.

"You no kill him?" asked the negro, who had regarded his companion's actions of the past half hour with evident disfavor.

"Not to-night," replied Ridge. "I am going to save him until morning. He will be stronger then, and in a better condition to afford us entertainment. Besides, I want time to think out the best way of doing it."

"To-morrow you kill him?" persisted the other.

"Perhaps. That is, if I have hit upon a good plan. Something novel and interesting, you know."

"You no kill him, me kill him," muttered Dionysio, as he sullenly began to make preparations for the night.

The remark, though not intended for the young American, still reached his ears and caused him a feeling of uneasiness.

"I believe you would, you black devil," he said to himself, "but you sha'n't commit your cowardly murder if I can help it." Then he again turned his attention to the prisoner, who was by this time sitting up and regarding his captors curiously.

"Are you going to kill me?" he asked, as Ridge rejoined him.

"No, of course not. What put such an idea into your head?"

".Because it so often happens that undesirable prisoners are disposed of in that way. You know I was ordered to have one shot only last night at just about this hour."

"Was it last night?" murmured Ridge. "It seems a month ago." Then he added, aloud, "Yes, I know, for I recognize you as Lieutenant Navarro, the officer who brought in the deserter, disposed of him according to General Pando's order, and then conducted me to prison."

"For which reason I should think you would now want to kill me," said the other, with a smile.

"We Americans are not in the habit of killing persons merely for obedience to orders."

"You are an American, then?"

"Yes," admitted Ridge, "and I thought you knew I was one."

"I was not certain, nor was the General, though he was determined to be on the safe side, and have you placed beyond a chance of making mischief."

"So I understood," laughed Ridge, "and for that reason I came away without waiting to say goodbye."

"Your escape raised an awful row," said the other, "and the General is furious over it. Swears he will hang every man, woman, or child connected with it if he discovers who aided you. Do you care to tell me how it was effected?"

"No," was the prompt reply, "I do not."

"I didn't suppose you would. At the same time I am greatly interested in it, especially as it caused me to be sent on my present mission. General Pando feared that you might make the same attempt at Jiguani as at Holguin. So I was ordered to get there first and have a reception prepared for you. Now, having failed to carry out his instructions, I do not know that I should dare present myself before him again, even if you should set me free, which, of course, is something not to be hoped for. What do you propose to do with me, anyway?"

"I don't know," replied Ridge, "but we will consider the situation after supper, which I see is ready."

The simple meal of roasted yams, which in war time was the principal article of food known to Cuban campaigners, was quickly eaten, and the two young men, already regarding each other more as friends than enemies, renewed their conversation.

"I am not anxious to resume my connection with

General Pando's army in any case," began Lieutenant Navarro, "since it is about to march against your countrymen, whom I esteem highly."

"Why?" asked Ridge. "Were you ever in my country?"

"Yes, and quite recently. You see, I have some distant cousins of my own name living in New Mexico, and only a year ago I paid them a visit. I was so charmed with the country, and so cordially welcomed, that I expressed a desire to remain with them and become a citizen of the United States. They encouraged the idea, and offered me an interest in a great ranch, where one of them, Maximilian by name, who is about my own age, proposed to become my partner. I accepted the offer, declared my intention of becoming a citizen before the proper authorities, and then returned to Spain to settle up my home affairs and procure money for my new undertaking.

"Unfortunately I had not served out my full military term, and before I could purchase exemption for the remaining time, there was a call for more troops to quell this miserable insurrection, and I was ordered with Blanco, the new Captain-General, to Cuba. Of course I don't mind fighting Cubans, whom I detest; but I do object to fighting against those whom I already consider as my adopted countrymen, especially as I have recently learned that the cousin with whom I was to go into business has joined the American army."

"Maximilian Navarro of New Mexico!" exclaimed

Ridge. "Why, I know him well. He is a captain in my own regiment, the First Volunteer Cavalry —the Rough Riders, as we are called. I saw him only five days ago, and hope soon to meet him again, before Santiago."

"Then are we friends rather than enemies!" cried the young Spaniard, grasping the other's hand, "and I will go with you to meet my cousin."

"Would you go as a deserter?"

"No, but as a prisoner of war under your protection."

"Of course," replied Ridge, who had just gained an inspiration. "A prisoner of war on parole, for you will give me your promise not to serve against the United States unless exchanged, will you not?"

"Most willingly," replied the other.

"But," continued Ridge, "if I take you to your cousin, I want you first to do me a favor."

"Gladly."

"And before I give you my whole confidence you must earn it."

"If it lies within my power, I will do so."

"Very good," said Ridge. "According to our laws, you are a citizen of the United States from having filed your intention to become one. Therefore, while not desiring you to fight against your native land, I am going to ask you to prove your loyalty to your adopted country by aiding my present mission."

"How may I do so?"

"By continuing your journey to Jiguani, delivering your despatches, which, by-the-way, I have examined; procuring for me a Spanish uniform, and meeting me two days later at Enramada. From there we will go together into Santiago, where you shall introduce me as your friend. Then will come my turn; for when the Americans land we will join them, and I shall take pleasure in presenting you to my friends as my friend. Will you undertake to do this?"

"Señor Teniente, I will," answered the young Spaniard, "and there is my hand on it. One thing, however, I must ask," he continued. "How will you deliver me from the hate of yonder black devil by the fire? But for you he would have taken my life long since, and when he discovers that you do not intend to kill me, he will assuredly make an attempt to do so."

"I have no doubt he would if he had a chance," replied Ridge, "but we must take turns at watching, and see that he doesn't get one. I will remain on guard the first half of the night, since you need sleep more than I, and will also show how fully I trust you by restoring your pistol."

"Your confidence will not be misplaced, señor."

With these arrangements perfected, the little camp sank into quiet, the only sounds being the chirping of insects, the harsh cries of night birds, and those made by the horses, which occasionally snorted at some fancied alarm. The two white men lay in their respective hammocks under the rude thatch of palm leaves, while Dionysio occupied a similar but smaller shelter beyond the fire.

For a long time Ridge watched the flicker of its flames, until they finally died down, and the darkness was only illumined by the fitful flashing of fireflies. As these were the most brilliant he had ever seen, his eyes followed their zig-zag dartings until they exercised a hypnotic influence, and his heavy breathing showed him to be fast asleep.

A few minutes later the occupant of the other hammock lifted his head and listened. Then he slipped noiselessly to the ground and disappeared in the profound darkness at the back of the hut. For an hour longer the peace of the camp was unbroken. At the end of that time one of the horses snorted more loudly than usual, while the other dropped heavily to the ground as though lying down.

After awhile, if Ridge had been awake, he might have noted a slight rustling in the grass, as though some animal were making a cautious way through it towards the hut. But his slumber was too profound to be easily broken, and no instinct warned him of approaching danger.

The rustling drew closer, until it sounded within a few feet of the unconscious sleeper. Then a black bulk slowly lifted from the ground, and gradually assumed the proportions of a man standing motionless. Of a sudden this figure, whose blurred outlines were barely discernible, made a quick movement, and the hammock of the young Spaniard was cut in twain by the sweeping blow of a machete.

At the same moment a pistol-shot rang out, followed by another and another. There was a smothered yell, a rush of feet, a brief struggle from the place where the horses were tethered, a crash, and directly afterwards Señorita, trembling in every limb, made her way to where her young master stood, as he had leaped from his hammock, dazed, and uncertain what to do.

## CHAPTER XVII

### IN THE HANDS OF SPANISH GUERILLAS

In addition to his alarm, Ridge was overcome with a guilty knowledge of having fallen asleep while on guard. Of course, he felt certain that he had only closed his eyes for a minute; but in that minute something dreadful, for which he was responsible, had happened. He had no idea what it was, but imagined the worst, and was greatly relieved to hear the voice of his prisoner-comrade at his side.

"What on earth—" he began; but just then Señorita dashed up to him in a state of terror, and for the moment demanded his attention. As he soothed her he called loudly for Dionysio, but there was no response.

"I am afraid he has escaped," said the young Spaniard, in rather a faint voice, from the ground, to which he had dropped exhausted by weakness and the intense strain of the past few hours. "He tried to kill me, you know."

"Tried to kill you!" exclaimed Ridge, incredulously. "But wait a moment. We must have a light. This darkness is awful."

Thus saying, he stepped to where a few coals of the camp-fire still smouldered, and began to throw on sticks, which, after a little coaxing, sprang into a bright blaze. By its light he detected two dark forms lying motionless a short distance away, and, with pistol held ready for action, went to discover their nature.

"Navarro must have been dreaming, or else greatly mistaken," he said to himself, "for here is Dionysio fast asleep. Come, wake up!" he cried aloud, at the same time prodding the prostrate form with his toe. As there was no response, he stooped to give the sleeper a vigorous shaking; but almost with the first touch he sprang back in horror. The man lay on his back, but with his head so twisted about that only its rear portion was visible, and Ridge instinctively knew that he was dead. The other motionless form was that of a dead horse, the one recently ridden by Lieutenant Navarro.

Having made this ghastly discovery, Ridge hastily returned to the hut to gain from his companion an explanation of what had happened.

"I could not sleep," said the young Spaniard, in answer to his inquiries, "though I lay still and tried hard to do so, until, by your heavy breathing, I discovered that you were no longer awake."

"I am awfully ashamed of myself," said Ridge.

"It is not to be wondered at," rejoined the other, consolingly. "You had not so much at stake as I, for only my life was threatened. Somehow, I felt certain that the black fiend who thirsted for my blood was also lying awake, and would make an attempt to kill me in my hammock before morning. So, without disturbing you, I moved to the back of the hut and waited for him. It must have been an hour before the horses began to give signs of great uneasiness, and then one of them fell. I suppose he must have killed it."

"Yes," said Ridge, "I reckon he did, since it now lies dead, and bleeding from a stab behind the left fore-shoulder."

"I imagined something of the kind," continued the other, "but still thought it safer for both of us not to disturb you. So I waited, more keenly alert than before, but heard nothing, until I saw him slowly rise and stand beside my hammock. The blow that he dealt it would have cut me in two had I still occupied it; and, with this discovery of his design, I fired three shots, one of which, I think, must have hit him. At any rate, he uttered a great cry and staggered away."

"After that," said Ridge, "he must have tried to escape on my horse, which probably flung him over her head and broke his neck. Didn't you, old girl?"

Had Señorita possessed the power of speech, she would certainly have answered "Yes," for that was exactly what had happened.

"At any rate," continued the young trooper, with a sigh of relief, "I am mighty glad my neglect of duty did not result more seriously. At the same time we are left in an awkward shape for continuing our journey."

"How so?" asked the other. "I am not afraid to walk."

"But I have lost my guide."

"You have lost one and gained another, who will serve you with equal skill, since I know very well the road to Jiguani."

"Of course you must know it," replied Ridge. "How stupid of me not to remember! and, as we can take turns at riding my horse, we shall doubtless get along all right."

There was no more sleep for either of the young soldiers that night; and by earliest dawn, having already eaten their frugal breakfast of roasted yams —an article of diet of which Ridge was becoming heartily tired—they set forth on the road to Jiguani.

As they were already on the southern slope of the mountains and descending into a broad valley, they made such rapid progress, by alternately riding and walking, that the sun had not passed its meridian when they reached the Cauto—the longest river in Cuba. There was formerly a small settlement at the crossing, but it had long since been destroyed, and now only presented the sight, so common in Cuba, of charred ruins devoid of human presence. There was neither bridge nor boat, but Lieutenant Navarro declared the river fordable at this point. Ridge regarded dubiously the chocolate-colored flood already swollen by the first of the summer rains, and wished that they had at least two horses with which to cross it. As they had not, and as nothing was to be gained by delay, he took his companion up behind him, and Señorita, thus doubly burdened, plunged bravely into the stream. Until they were half-way across all went well, the mare cautiously feeling her way, and the water not reaching more than to her belly. Then, without warning, she dropped into a hole so deep that the turbid current closed above the heads of her riders as well as her own.

Reappearing on the surface, the mare struck out for shore, with Ridge swimming beside her, and the young Spaniard, who was a poor swimmer, clinging desperately to her tail. Fortunately the channel into which they had plunged was so narrow that within two minutes they had reached its farther side in safety, and could once more touch bottom. Wading up-stream to a point where the road left the river, they emerged from the water, soaked and dripping, but thankful to have met with no worse harm than a ducking.

As Ridge turned to laugh at the forlorn appearance presented by his companion, the latter uttered an exclamation of dismay, and at the same moment they were surrounded by half a dozen as villanous-looking ruffians as our troopers had yet seen in Cuba. His heart sank within him. Again was he a prisoner with the prospect at least of having his journey seriously delayed. In the confusion of the moment he did not note that those into whose hands he had fallen wore blouses and trousers of blue drilling traversed by narrow, vertical stripes of white,

the campaign uniform of the Spanish army in Cuba;
but his companion instantly recognized it, and demanded, with a tone of authority, "Who commands here?"

"I do," replied the most ill-favored of the crew, stepping forward.

"You are a guerilla, are you not?"

"A captain of irregular cavalry, señor. And you?"

"I," replied the lieutenant, "am a major of regulars, attached to the staff of General Luis Pando, and on an urgent mission to Jiguani. My horse was killed by insurgents this morning, and I had a narrow escape, leaving one of them dead."

"Which is the reason that two of you rode one horse in crossing the river, and so led me to mistake you for 'mamby?'"* said the guerilla captain.

"Very likely, sir, though I can't be accountable for your mistakes. Now you may let your men make a fire by which we can dry ourselves, and you may also have food prepared, for we are hungry."

"But your friend, Major, who is he?" asked the other, scanning Ridge's brown canvas uniform doubtfully.

"None of your business, sir. Let it be sufficient that he is my friend, and do as I bid you without further words."

At this Discipline, even though suspicious, yielded to the voice of Authority, and the guerilla made

* Derisive term applied by Spaniards to Cuban insurgents.

surly announcement that both fire and food were close at hand.

This proved true; for, on gaining the face of the bluff, our friends found themselves in the presence of some twenty more guerillas, who were gathered about fires, cooking and eating strips of meat from a recently butchered steer. Their horses were picketed close at hand, and beyond them grazed a herd of small wild-looking Cuban cattle. For these this detachment of "beef-riders" had scoured the country-side, and they were now returning with them to Jiguani. A scout from this party, patrolling the river-bank, had notified the captain that strangers were about to cross from the other side, and he had thus been enabled to prepare for their reception.

He was evidently disappointed that they and their belongings could not be seized as prizes of war, and manifested this by the envious glances that he cast at Señorita as well as upon the weapons that Ridge was drying and cleaning. Especially was the young trooper's rifle an object of longing admiration, and, after a critical examination, the captain even went so far as to offer to buy it; but Ridge refused to part with the gun, whereupon the man turned sulky, and declined to hold further intercourse with him.

After a while the whole party again took the road, Lieutenant Navarro riding a spare horse that he had "requisitioned" from the guerilla leader. The latter rode with his guests at the head of the advance-guard, and Ridge noticed that, as two scouts were still in front of them, while others of the guerillas rode on either side, they were completely surrounded, and practically prisoners. He suggested as much to his companion, but the latter only smiled, and said:

"What matters it, so long as we are safely escorted to Jiguani?"

"But I don't want to go there."

"True. I had forgotten. You wish to proceed to Enramada, where I am to join you."

"Yes, on the second day from now."

"With only slight delay we might travel together."

"I have reasons for preferring to go alone."

"You will be in danger from the Cubans."

"Ask your guerilla captain if he thinks so."

The latter said he did not believe there were any insurgents on the Enramada road just then, since their chief, General Garcia, had withdrawn from Bayamo, and was understood to be collecting his entire force near El Cobre, in the Sierra Maestra, or southern coast range.

"Very well, then," said Ridge. "I desire to leave you as soon as we come to the Enramada road, and I wish that you would inform your guerilla friend that I propose to do so."

"I will do better; for when we reach the forks, which will be shortly, I will order you to take the one to the left, while we keep to the right, and he will not dare attempt to detain you."

But the guerilla, who had determined to possess himself of Ridge's horse and rifle, did dare do that very thing. Thus, when at the forking of the roads the order was given as proposed, and Ridge started to obey it, the captain whipped out a pistol, and declared that the stranger must accompany him into Jiguani for examination before the authorities.

At this our young trooper clapped spurs to Señorita, flung himself flat on her back, and dashed away on his chosen road, followed by a scattering volley of pistol-shots, and by four of the best mounted among the guerillas, who, at their captain's command, sprang after him in hot pursuit.

## CHAPTER XVIII

### DEATH OF SEÑORITA

FROM the earliest days of Spanish rule in Cuba human life has been held very cheap. Especially of late years, when thousands of men, women, and children have been wantonly murdered, has the killing of a man for any reason been lightly regarded. So in the present instance the guerilla captain instructed those detailed to overtake the escaping prisoner to kill him and bring back all his property. It seemed to him an easy task for his well-mounted beef-riders, familiar with every foot of that region, to overtake and overpower one who had already travelled far that day, and was evidently a stranger to the country. When they had done so he would obtain that coveted rifle. On the whole, he was glad that one of his prisoners had made a foolish dash for liberty, and rather wished the other would do the same thing.

But the other contented himself with denouncing the action of the guerilla captain in bitter terms, and promising to report it the moment they reached the Spanish lines. At all of which the latter only smiled contemptuously.

In the mean time Ridge, lying low on his horse's neck to offer as small a target as possible to the shots fired by his pursuers whenever they sighted him, was uttering words of encouragement in Señorita's ear, and she was responding with such a burst of speed that the beef-riders were quickly left far behind. At length nothing was to be seen or heard of them; and, believing that they had given over the chase as hopeless, the young trooper allowed the panting mare who had borne him so bravely to slacken her heading pace until it was reduced to a walk.

He was still in the broad Cauto valley, where the sabanetas, or open glades of tall grasses, were interspersed with wide tracts of impenetrable jungle and forests of palms. By these his view was limited on every side, but he knew that the mountains among which he hoped to find the insurgent leader lay to the southward. So he determined to leave the road by the first trail leading in that direction, and continue on it until he should meet some one willing to guide him to his destination.

Having formed this crude plan, and believing that Señorita had been allowed sufficient time to recover her breath, he began to urge her to a better speed, but, to his surprise, she failed to respond. Neither words nor spur served to move her from the slow walk into which she had fallen. Such a thing had not happened since the beginning of their acquaintance in far-away San Antonio, and the young trooper dismounted to discover what had gone wrong.

He had not far to look, for, as he touched the ground, a red trickle of blood caught his eye. The plucky little mare had been hit by one of the beef-riders' shots, but had given no sign until now, when her weakness could no longer be overcome. So copious was the flow of blood that it was evident an artery had been severed, and already had the loss been very great. In vain did Ridge strive to stanch the cruel outspurt. He had no proper appliances, and the evil was too serious to be remedied by his simple skill. Even as he made the attempt the gallant beast swayed, staggered, and then sank with a groan to the ground. Almost sobbing with grief and dismay, Ridge flung himself beside her and threw an arm caressingly across her neck.

"Poor old girl! Dear old girl!" he cried. "To think that I should have brought you here just for this. It is too bad! too bad! And what shall I do without you?"

Then with a sudden thought he sprang to his feet and began an eager search on both sides of the road for water, but found none. Disappointed and heavy-hearted, he returned to Señorita. She lay as he had left her, but motionless and with closed eyes. Again he knelt at her side, and at the sound of his voice the loving eyes were once more opened. At the same time, with a mighty effort, the proud head was uplifted, as though the mare were about to struggle to her feet. Just then came a shot from behind them, and, with a bullet intended for her young master buried deep in her brain, the dear horse yielded up her life.

The shot was so instantly followed by a clatter of hoofs, that Ridge had barely time to snatch his rifle and fling himself to the ground behind Señorita's body before the beef-riders appeared charging up the road, yelling and firing as they came.

With his rifle resting across the mare's side, Ridge took quick aim and fired. One of the advancing horsemen threw up his arms and fell over backward, but the young American did not see him; for, without waiting to note the effect of his shot, he dropped the rifle and seized his revolver. It was a self-cocking weapon, and as rapidly as he could pull the trigger he delivered the contents of all six chambers at the guerillas. Whether or not they fired in return he did not know, but as the smoke from his own fusillade cleared away he saw one man lying motionless in the road, and another dragging himself into the grass at one side. From that direction also came the furious plunging of a horse. Of the others who had pursued him nothing was to be seen. Hastily reloading his revolver, and throwing another cartridge into the chamber of his rifle, Ridge nervously awaited further developments. Would they again charge upon his front, or would they seek to outflank him by crawling through the dense growth on either side? The latter would be the safer move, and could be easily made.

As our young soldier realized this, he decided to

forestall the attempt by taking to the grass himself, and in another moment he was cautiously creeping on hands and knees amid the hot brown stalks that grew many feet above his head. Fearing that his movement might attract attention, he did not go far; but, after making his way for a few rods parallel to the road, he again gained its edge and halted at a place where, peering between the grass stems, he could see his dead horse.

Here he lay motionless until he became convinced that his enemies had beaten a retreat and would trouble him no more. Thus thinking, impatient of delay, and painfully cramped by his position, he was about to rise when the long silence was broken by a low cuckoo call close at hand. Was it a signal or the note of some strange bird? As Ridge hesitated, the call was answered from the other side of the road. Again it sounded from the side on which he lay; then, from the opposite side a man's head came slowly into view, low down among the grass stems. After hasty glances both up and down the road it was withdrawn, and the cuckoo notes were again exchanged. Then two of the baffled beef-riders rose boldly to their feet and stepped out in full view, close beside the dead horse. The young trooper could not distinguish their words; but, from their angry gestures, they were discussing his disappearance and the advisability of a further attempt to capture him.

At the same moment his own thoughts were of a most conflicting nature. One of the men was covered by his rifle, and his finger was on its ready trigger, but he hesitated to pull it. They had killed his horse and sought to take his life. Even now they would shoot him down without mercy, and as a pastime, if the opportunity offered. Knowing this, and realizing his danger if those men should discover him, the young American still hesitated to fire from ambush and take human life in cold blood.

That others did not feel as he did about such things was shown while he hesitated, for the two beef-riders had been in sight but a few seconds when there came a flash and a roar of guns from the opposite side of the road, a little beyond where Ridge was hiding. Both the guerillas fell as though struck by a thunder-bolt, and their blue-clad forms lay motionless across Señorita's body. Her death was amply avenged.

At this startling demonstration in his behalf, Ridge sprang to his feet in full view of half a dozen men, ragged and swarthy, who were running down the road with yells of delight. They halted at sight of the stranger, and some raised their weapons; but he, recognizing them as Cubans, called out: "I am Americano, and those Spaniards whom you have so bravely killed sought my life. Viva Cuba libre!"

Upon this they again advanced with shouts and eager questions. They belonged to a detachment of the Cuban army on its way to join General Garcia, and had been attracted by the sound of firing. Coming to discover its cause, they had seen the dead horse, and were stealing cautiously towards it when halted by the familiar cuckoo call of their enemies.

That Ridge had suffered at the hands of the Spaniards, and fought with them, was a sufficient passport to their favor. Thus when he explained his desire to meet their general they consented to guide him to the Cuban rendezvous, which they said was high up in the mountains.

With a heavy heart and tear-dimmed eyes the young American turned from a last look at his beloved horse, and set forth with these new acquaintances on their toilsome march. He carried only his arms, but the Cubans had stripped the dead—both men and horses—of everything valuable, and were thus well laden with trophies.

A short distance from the spot where Señorita had given her own life in saving that of her master, they turned into a barely discernible trail that soon brought them to the foot-hills, where they camped for the night. All the next day they pushed on, with infrequent halts, ever climbing higher over trails so rough and obscure that only experienced eyes could follow them. Here and there they passed food-stations guarded by old men, poorly clad women, and naked children. Each of these consisted of a thatched hut, an open fire, and a sweet-potato patch, and to the marching Cubans they supplied roasted potatoes, sugar-cane, and occasionally a few ripe mangoes.

Ridge and a guide, to whom he had promised

money, outstripped the others, and shortly before sunset of the second day reached the summit of a pass lying between the great bulk of El Cobre on the east and Pico Turquino, the tallest mountain in Cuba. From this point was outspread a superb view of densely wooded mountain slopes tumbling steeply down to the boundless blue of the Caribbean Sea. Here the guide departed, promising shortly to return, leaving Ridge to gaze upon the wonderful panorama unfolded on all sides, and thrilled with the thought that he had crossed Cuba.

While he stood thus, forgetful of everything save the marvellous beauty of his surroundings, he was puzzled by a sound as of distant thunder coming from a direction in which no cloud was visible. As he speculated concerning this phenomenon, he was startled by a voice close at hand saying, in English: "That is a welcome sound to Cuban ears, señor, since it is the thunder of American war-ships bombarding the defences of Santiago."

## CHAPTER XIX

### CALIXTO GARCIA THE CUBAN

"THE thunder of American war-ships!" Instantly, as Ridge learned its nature, the mighty sound took on a new significance, and seemed like the voice of his own glorious country demanding freedom for an oppressed people. Filled with this thought, he turned to the man who had suggested it, and found himself in the presence of one wearing the uniform of a Cuban officer. The latter had taken off his hat, and the young American noted a livid bullet scar in the centre of his broad white forehead. The man was elderly, fine-looking, and smooth-shaven except for a heavy white mustache. His picture had been published in every illustrated paper and magazine in the United States.

Promptly giving a military salute, Ridge said, "I believe I have the honor of addressing General Garcia."

"Yes, I am Calixto Garcia. But who are you?"

"An officer of the American army, come to you with a message from its commanding General."

"Have you credentials or despatches by which you may be known?"

"Only this, sir." Here Ridge lowered his voice and gave, for the second time since landing in Cuba, the secret countersign of the Junta.

"It is sufficient," said the General, smiling and holding out his hand. "Now what is your message?"

"That the American army of invasion, having sailed from Tampa, is due within the next two days to arrive off Santiago; and General Shafter, who commands it, is desirous of an interview with you before landing his troops. He asks you to name the place of meeting."

"Thank you, sir, for bringing me this great news, and gladly will I meet your General whenever he may choose to come. Also I will fix the place of meeting down yonder at Aserraderos. From this station I will watch day and night for his ships, and when they come will be ready to receive him."

"Very good, sir. I will so report to my General."

"But how do you expect to communicate with him?" asked Garcia, curiously.

"I propose to go from here to Enramada, to which place I was about to ask you to favor me with a mount and a guide. At that point I have arranged to meet a friend who will give me Spanish protection, and under whose escort I shall visit Santiago. After that I shall be guided by circumstances. But if I live I shall certainly be at Daiquiri in time to meet the American army."

"You have undertaken a difficult task, and I only hope it may be accomplished," replied the General, thoughtfully. "Of course I will furnish you with a horse and an escort to Enramada, which place, as you are doubtless aware, is already occupied by my men."

"By the Cubans?" cried Ridge, in dismay.

"Certainly. We drove out the Spaniards several days ago, and have advanced our lines to within a few miles of Santiago. At present that city is surrounded on three sides by the forces of Generals Castillo and Rabi."

"In that case, sir, I shall ask for protection to the extreme limit of the Cuban lines, both for myself and my friend."

"Is he a Spaniard?" asked Garcia, suspiciously.

"He is an American citizen," replied Ridge, "though at present appearing as a Spaniard, and wearing the uniform of a Spanish officer."

"What is his name?"

"He is travelling under the name of Ramon Navarro."

"Very Spanish indeed, and he could not have done a more reckless or foolish thing than attempt to pass himself off as a Spaniard in this part of the island. If he is discovered near Enramada he will undoubtedly be killed without a chance to explain who he really is. But that is the way with you Americans. Confident in your own ignorance, you are always pushing ahead without stopping to count the cost."

"At the same time we generally get there."

"Get where?" asked the other, sharply.

"To the place we start for."

"Oh yes, you get there, in some shape, though perhaps sorry that you have done so. In the present campaign, for instance, I have no doubt that the very first Americans landed will make a dash for Santiago, without waiting for artillery or even provisions. If they win a victory, it will be by the good fortune that often attends fools; but the chances are that when they enter Santiago it will be as prisoners of war."

"Sir!" cried Ridge, "I am an American, and an officer in the American army."

"Pardon, señor; I forgot," replied the General. "I was allowing myself to utter aloud my thoughts, a thing extremely wrong and ill-advised. I have really no doubt in the world that your gallant countrymen will conduct themselves most admirably. Now if you will come to my poor camp I will make you as comfortable as possible for the night, and in the morning we will decide what is best for you to do."

"Thank you, sir," said our young trooper, "but with your permission I should prefer to make a start at once, with the hope of reaching Enramada before my comrade, and thus preventing a sad mistake on the part of your troops."

"But, my young friend, you have already travelled far to-day and are exhausted."

"I still have some strength left."

"Night is upon us, and the trails are very dangerous."

"There is a young moon, and you will furnish reliable guides," replied Ridge, smiling.

"If I should not furnish them?"

"Then I would set forth alone."

"You are determined, then, to proceed at once?"

"I am, sir, unless detained by force."

"Ah, heavens! These Americans!" cried the General, with an air of resignation. "They will leave nothing for to-morrow that may be squeezed into to-day. They know not the meaning of 'mañana.' Ever impatient, ever careless of consequences, and yet they succeed. Can it be that theirs is the way of wisdom? But no, it is their good fortune, what they call 'luck.' Yes, señor, it shall be as you desire. In an hour all shall be in readiness for your departure."

"Couldn't you make it half an hour, General?" asked Ridge, with an audacity that drew forth only a grunt from the Cuban leader.

So it happened that in something less than an hour from the time of this important interview our young American, well fed, and provided with a pass through the Cuban lines for himself and one friend, was retracing his steps down the northern slope of the Sierra Maestra. He was mounted on a rawbacked but sure-footed Cuban pony, and escorted by half a dozen ragged cavalrymen. They had barely started before he was thankful that he had not attempted to make the journey unguided; nor had they gone a mile before he knew that he could never have accomplished it alone. Often he found himself traversing narrow trails on the brink of black space where a single misstep would have brought his career to a sudden termination. Again he passed through gloomy tunnels of dense foliage, slid down precipitous banks, only to plunge into rushing, bowlder-strewn torrents at the bottom, and scramble up slopes of slippery clay on the farther side. All this was done by the feeble and ever-lessening light of a moon in its first quarter, and as it finally sank out of sight the leader of the escort called a halt, declaring that they could not move another rod before daybreak.

Thus Ridge was forced to take a few hours of rest, and so exhausted was he that his companions had difficulty in rousing him at dawn. Again they pushed forward, shivering in the chill of early morning, and blistered by the sun's fervent heat a few hours later, until ten o'clock found them on the grass-grown highway leading from Santiago to Bayamo, and a few miles west of Enramada. Here, as Ridge believed himself to be well in advance of his comrade, he decided to await his coming. At the same time he sent one of his escort into Enramada to discover if Lieutenant Navarro had by any chance reached that place, and to arrange for fresh mounts. Then he threw himself down in the scant shadow of a thorny bush for a nap.

Apparently his companions, who had promised to keep a close watch of the highway, did the same thing, for when he next awoke it was with a start and the consciousness that a horseman was dashing past at full speed on the road to Enramada.

In less than a minute the shamefaced squad was in hot pursuit, but though they strove to atone for their neglect of duty by furious riding, they did not overtake the horseman until they discovered him halted by an outpost, who allowed him to pass as they came in sight. When they in turn were halted they learned that the man whom they had followed so briskly was a Cuban scout just in from a tour of observation.

So Ridge rode slowly into Enramada, reported to the officer in command, and remained in that wretched village until nightfall in a state of nervous impatience. He was most anxious to push forward, since every minute was now of value, but could not desert the friend whom he had promised to meet at this place. He feared that without his protection Navarro would come to grief among the Cubans, and also he was depending upon the young Spaniard for a safe entry into Santiago.

At length dusk had fallen. The impatient young trooper had eaten a supper of tough bull-beef and "those everlasting yams," as he called them, with his Cuban friends, and was pacing restlessly to and fro a short distance beyond a camp-fire, about which they smoked their cigarettes, when a ragged, slouch-hatted figure approached him.

"Señor Americano."

"Well, what do you want?"

"If Don José Remelios desires the company of Ramon Navarro into Santiago, I am ready."

"Good Heavens, man!"

"Hush! Tell them you can wait no longer. Set forth alone, follow the railroad, and I will meet you."

Then, before Ridge could reply, the figure darted away and was lost in the night shadows.

Fifteen minutes later the young American, despite the polite protests of his entertainers, had left Enramada, dismissed the escort who had passed him through the Cuban pickets, declined further guidance, on the plea that he could not get lost while following the railway, and was watching anxiously for the appearance of his friend.

Suddenly he was confronted by a motionless horseman dimly seen on the embankment ahead of him, and in another minute the comrades were exchanging greetings.

"How did you reach Enramada without my knowledge?" asked Ridge, finally. "I have watched every moving creature in the place since noon."

"Slipped in, disguised by this horrible Cuban costume, after dark," laughed Navarro. "Shouldn't have come at all but for my promise, and a recollection that I was a prisoner of war on parole, since I learned at Jiguani that Enramada was occupied by the insurgents."

"But I have a pass for you from Garcia himself."

"Even had I known it I should not have ventured among those who might have recognized me; for where a Spaniard is concerned, any Cuban will kill him first and examine his pass afterwards."

"I suppose that is so," replied Ridge, with a memory of del Concha. "Anyhow, I am mighty glad everything is turning out so well. Now, hurrah for Santiago, and the American army that is to capture it!"

"Do you believe they can do it?"

"Of course I do," was the confident answer.

But a few hours later, when from a wooded hilltop he looked down upon the widespread city in which were quartered 10,000 veteran troops, protected by strong intrenchments, formidable batteries, and by Admiral Cervera's powerful squadron, he wondered if, after all, his countrymen had not undertaken a task far more difficult than they imagined.

CHAPTER XX

THE TWO ADMIRALS

IT was a glorious morning, and a glorious sight was disclosed by the rising sun — a palm-shaded city of red-tiled roofs, dominated by a fine, double-towered cathedral, and a broad, land-locked bay set in a circle of rounded hills and rugged mountains. On the placid bosom of the bay rode Cervera's proud squadron of war-ships—five mighty cruisers, four of which were of the latest model and most approved armament; two wicked-looking torpedo-boat destroyers, each claimed to be more than a match for any battle-ship afloat, and a few gun-boats that had been used for coast patrol. From the war-ships came the cherry notes of bugles, and from the Plaza de Armas, in which a regiment was passing in review, swelled the inspiring music of a full military band. Beyond the city every near-by elevation was occupied by a stout block-house, each displaying the red and yellow flag of Spain, and forming the nucleus for radiating lines of rifle-pits. Far down at the entrance to the bay rose the grim walls of Santiago's Morro Castle, and beyond it floated against the blue sky soft smoke clouds that

Ridge felt sure must come from the American ships on blockade.

This was Santiago. This the peaceful scene that was soon to be transformed into a battle-field. Here, within a few days, victory and defeat would meet face to face. Which side would claim the former? Until this moment Ridge had never doubted. He had often heard the boast that his own regiment could drive every Spaniard out of Cuba, and had believed it. Now he knew that here alone was work cut out for an army.

These reflections of our young trooper were interrupted by his companion, who said, "It is a wonderful picture; but I am too hungry to gaze on it any longer; so let us hasten into the city, with the hope of finding a breakfast."

Both the young men wore Spanish uniforms that Navarro had brought with him, and, protected by these, they rode boldly down to the nearest outpost. Here the lieutenant demanded that they be conducted to headquarters, to which they were accordingly sent under guard.

Many of the narrow streets through which they passed were indescribably filthy, but these became cleaner as they neared the Casa Municipal. Here they were graciously received by General Linares, to whom they were presented by one of his staff, who recognized Navarro as a friend. The General complimented them on having eluded the Cubans, and was much gratified to learn that Pando's army was on its way from Holguin to reinforce him.

After a few minutes of conversation, during which he promised to give both of them details for field duty, he dismissed them, and they were at liberty to accept an invitation to breakfast at the San Carlos Club.

In the cool club-house, which faces the Plaza de Armas, where the band plays in the evening and fountains plash softly amid blossoming shrubbery, Ridge and his companion were introduced to many officers, a number of whom were from the war-ships.

Santiago was very dull just then; its communication with the outside world was cut off. No ships could enter its beautiful harbor, business was almost at a standstill, and there was little to talk about. So the advent of two strangers into the club was hailed with joy, and they were plied with questions. No one seemed to suspect that our young American was other than what he professed to be, though his answers to many of their questions were necessarily vague and unsatisfactory. In order to entertain them, the resident officers proposed various trips to places of near-by interest, such as the fortifications, the barracks where Lieutenant Hobson of the American navy was confined, the Morro, from which a view of the blockading squadron could be had, or to the Spanish war-ships lying in the harbor, the last of which was accepted for that morning.

As soon, therefore, as breakfast was over, the new-comers were escorted to the water-front, where lay several steam-launches. As they reached the landing-place a fine-looking man, white bearded, with twinkling eyes and kindly features, drove up in a carriage, and alighting with springy step, was instantly saluted by every officer present. He acknowledged the courtesy by lifting his hat and speaking to several of them, whom he called by name. Emboldened by his kindness, these ventured to present the new arrivals and mention their desire to visit the Spanish ships; whereupon Admiral Cervera, bravest and most chivalrous of Spain's commanders, promptly invited them to accompany him to the flag-ship.

As they steamed down the bay in the superbly appointed launch flying an Admiral's flag and manned by a picked crew in snowy duck, Ridge sat silent, in a very confused frame of mind, and paying scant attention to the gay conversation carried on by the other members of the party. He had been overcome by the courtesy of his reception in Santiago, and was feeling keenly the meanness of his position.

"I'll be shot for disobedience of orders before I ever again undertake to act the low-down part of a spy," he reflected, bitterly. At the same time he was wondering how he should manage to escape the kindly but embarrassing attentions of these new-found friends, and reach Daiquiri in time to communicate with General Shafter upon his arrival.

In spite of these thoughts, he did not fail to admire the beauty and massive symmetry of the ships they were approaching. There lay the *Cristobal Colon*, latest product of Italian skill; the splendid *Vizcaya*, that had recently attracted the admiration of all who saw her in New York Harbor; the *Almirante Oquendo*, that had been received with such wild enthusiasm in Havana; the *Maria Teresa*, famed for the richness of her interior fittings; the *Reina Mercedes*, used as a hospital-ship; the *Pluton* and the *Furor*, low, black, and ugly to look upon, both holding records for enormous speed, and more dreaded as engines of destruction than all the others put together. Stripped to fighting trim, these ships were the very embodiment of modern sea-power, and in his ignorance Ridge wondered if anything afloat could resist them. From them his attention was at length attracted to the Admiral, who was saying:

"I am about to send this launch, under a flag of truce, out to the American flag-ship to procure some supplies for our prisoners, the Señor Hobson and his men. So if you have a desire to view the Yankee ships at close range I shall be pleased to have you accompany it. Possibly you speak the English, in which case you might prove of use as interpreter."

"I do not speak it so well as does my friend the Señor Remelios," replied Lieutenant Navarro, to whom this invitation had been extended.

"Then it may be that he will do me the favor to accompany the launch," suggested the Admiral, and of course Ridge gladly embraced the opportunity **thus** offered.

"Perhaps I can stay on board the American ship," he said to himself, "and not be compelled to revisit Santiago until I can do so as an honest fighter, instead of as a contemptible spy. And what a chance it will be for Navarro to escape from the Spaniards!"

Half an hour later the trim launch, now displaying a large white flag forward, had passed the masts of the sunken *Merrimac*, the frowning Morro on its lofty headland, and, standing out to sea, was drawing near the superb cruiser *New York*, flag-ship of Admiral Sampson's fleet. On either side of her, in imposing array, lay the great battle-ships *Iowa*, *Massachusetts*, *Texas*, and *Oregon*, the last of which had recently hurried to the scene of conflict from San Francisco, making a record voyage of 13,000 miles by way of Cape Horn. Besides these there was the *Brooklyn*, swiftest of American cruisers, together with half a dozen more—cruisers, gunboats, yachts, and torpedo-boats—all in war-paint, all ready for instant action, and all flying the banner of stars and stripes. At the wonderful sight Ridge's heart glowed with patriotism and a new courage. How impregnable looked the huge battle-ships!— how terrible! Nothing could withstand them! He felt sure of that.

The young Spaniard who sat beside him gazed on the outspread American fleet in silent amazement. He had thought Cervera's ships formidable, but now it seemed to him they would be but playthings for these modern leviathans.

As the Spanish launch ranged alongside the flag-ship, an object of curious attention to all on board, it was courteously received; but, to Ridge's disappointment, only the officer in charge was permitted to leave it. A few minutes later, however, a cadet tripped lightly down the side ladder to say that the gentleman who spoke English was requested to report on deck. As in obedience to this order our young trooper followed him up the ladder, he found opportunity to say in a low but earnest voice:

"I must see the Admiral, alone if possible. Have important communication for him. Try and arrange an interview."

The cadet looked back in surprise, and then nodded his head. The next moment they were on deck, when the "Señor Remelios" could barely control his joyful emotions at finding himself once more among his countrymen and beneath his country's flag.

After a brief transaction of business the guests were invited into the ward-room, which they had scarcely entered when word was passed that the one speaking English was again wanted on deck. Promptly obeying this summons, Ridge was conducted to a large after-cabin which he found occupied by two officers. One, with stern features, iron-gray beard, deeply lined forehead, and piercing eyes, he instantly recognized as Admiral Sampson. The other he guessed to be Captain Chadwick, commander of the ship.

"Well, sir," began the former, sharply, as the

new-comer was left standing, cap in hand, before them, "I understand that you wish to make a private communication of importance. What is it? Are you desirous of deserting your countrymen and joining us? If so, I would advise you to go elsewhere before declaring your intention, because on board this ship we have very little sympathy for deserters."

"Seeing that I am an American soldier, sir, belonging to Colonel Wood's First Volunteer Cavalry, and am here by special order from General Miles, I don't think there is much danger that I shall desert," replied Ridge.

Both of his hearers uttered exclamations as he announced his nationality, and Captain Chadwick muttered, "I should never have suspected it."

At that moment Ridge caught sight of his own face in a mirror, the first he had seen in two weeks, and was startled to note how very Spanish he looked.

In a few minutes he had explained the situation, and given General Garcia's message appointing Aserraderos as a meeting-place to the American commander. When his report was finished, he added: "Now, sir, can't I remain here until the army arrives? I never realized until to-day how humiliating it is to be a spy."

"I wish I might say yes," replied Admiral Sampson, meditatively, "but fear I cannot. According to your own account, you have not completed your mission by making a study of the condition and defences of Santiago, upon which you are to report to the commander of the first American force that lands. Also, I could not detain one who comes as a Spanish officer under flag of truce, without making things very unpleasant for such of our men as are held prisoners by the enemy. You must not think of your position as humiliating, but as one of great importance and responsibility, as well as of great danger. You say, too, that you have a Spanish friend in the launch who wishes to remain here with you, and whom you cannot desert, but I certainly could not receive him under the circumstances. Therefore, much as I regret to say so, it seems to me that both my duty and yours point to your return by the way you came."

As Ridge, admitting the justice of this decision, was about to take his leave, the executive officer of the ship entered hastily and reported:

"A heavy smoke to the eastward, sir, believed to be that of the transports bringing General Shafter's army."

## CHAPTER XXI

A SPANIARD'S LOYALTY

BOTH officers sprang to their feet at the startling announcement that the eagerly awaited but long delayed transports were in sight, and Admiral Sampson extended his hand to Ridge, saying:

"Go back to Santiago and your duty, my boy. I will convey your report concerning the meeting with Garcia to General Shafter."

Then all hurried to the deck, and in another minute the great war-ship had started eastward to welcome the troops, while the Spanish launch, which had been hastily dismissed, was heading towards Santiago Bay with every member of the party she had brought out still on board.

"What is about to happen?" asked one of the Spanish officers, in bewilderment.

"The ships bringing the American army have been sighted," replied Ridge, who saw no reason for withholding information that must soon be known to every one.

Upon this there was great excitement in the launch, which was pressed to its utmost speed, that the news might be carried to Admiral Cervera and General Linares as quickly as possible.

At his own request, Ridge, in company with Lieutenant Navarro, was permitted to carry it to the General, who said, quietly :

" Very good, gentlemen ; and now, since the time for action has arrived, I will assign you to the important duty of patrolling the coast, from which you will bring to me, at Sevilla, earliest word of any attempted landing by the enemy. You will act independently, but in co-operation with Captain del Rey, who is already scouting in the neighborhood of Guantanamo with his company of cavalry. It is supposed that the landing will be made there, but— as Heaven only knows what these Yankees may do —we must watch every possible point."

Nothing could have suited Ridge better than this; and a few minutes later, with Santiago left behind, he and his companion were galloping in the direction of the Morro, from whose lofty walls they would be able to command a vast sweep of ocean and coast. Already were its garrison crowding tower and battlement to gaze wonderingly at the American fleet coming from the eastward. A double column eight miles long of ships, crowded to their utmost capacity with armed men, was advancing under low-trailing banners of black smoke, like a resistless fate. As they neared the war-ships, that had for a month impatiently awaited them, these thundered forth a welcome from their big guns. Bands played, swift steam-launches darted to and fro, and a mighty volume of cheering from twice ten thousand throats was borne to those who listened on land like the roar of a breaking tempest. The American army and navy had met at last, and were joined in a common cause.

For an hour our young trooper watched with swelling heart this wonderful meeting of his countrymen. Then he had the satisfaction of seeing one of the transports steam away to the westward in the direction of Aserraderos. While his companions asked one another the meaning of this manœuvre, he believed it to indicate that the meeting between Generals Shafter and Garcia, for which he had arranged, was about to be effected.

As it was evident that no landing was to be attempted that day, the young men so reported to General Linares at Sevilla, where they also spent the night. Another day of suspense and anxious waiting was passed, with the American transports rolling idly in the offing, and making no effort to discharge their human freight. At the same time the war-ships kept the Spaniards in a state of feverish excitement by shelling every place along twenty miles of coast where a landing might be made.

A swarm of Spanish scouts watched these operations from the hill-tops, and at short intervals during the day reported the enemy's movements to General Linares ; but of them all none was so active as Ridge and his companion. From earliest dawn until dark they scoured the country lying adjacent to the coast, gaining a complete knowledge of its so-called roads, which were but the roughest of trails, only intended for saddle or pack animals, and of its defences. They also made such full reports to headquarters of everything that was going on as to completely win the confidence of the Spanish commander. Consequently he was not prepared to accept, without further proof, the abrupt statement made by a major of his staff, that one of his favorite scouts was an American, and probably a spy.

It was the second day after the arrival of the transports. The two officers were alone in the room occupied by General Linares as an office, and from it Ridge had just departed after making a report to the effect that he had not yet seen anything indicating the selection of a landing-place on the part of the enemy.

"What makes you think him an American?" asked the General.

"Because," replied the Major, "I have recognized him. His face was familiar from the first, and when I saw him ride I knew that I had also seen him ride before, but could not tell where. Only now has it come to me, and I know that in Yokohama I saw him within a year win the great hurdle-race of the English and American residents."

"Even that would not make him an American."

"It was everywhere proclaimed that he was such."

"Are you certain that this is the same man?"

"I am certain. I now also recall his name. It was Norreese—the Señor Norreese."

"But he was introduced by Lieutenant Navarro, who is known to every one, and whose loyalty is beyond question."

"Did Lieutenant Navarro know him in Spain?"

"I will ask him."

So an orderly was despatched to request Lieutenant Navarro to report immediately at headquarters.

The two friends were eating a hasty lunch when this message reached them, and Ridge had just announced his intention to start for Daiquiri as soon as it was finished. He alone knew that the American landing would be made there, and he wished to be on hand when it was effected. Navarro had arranged to go with him, and both were impatient of the delay promised by the General's order.

"It is too bad!" exclaimed Ridge; "for we ought to be there now, since they may already be landing. I hope the General doesn't want to send us off in some other direction."

"For fear that he may," said the other, "you had better start at once towards Daiquiri, and I will follow the moment I am at liberty to do so."

"That's good advice," repeated Ridge, "and I will do as you suggest."

With this understanding, and having arranged a place of meeting, the young trooper set forth on his twelve-mile ride over the narrow trails of the broken and densely wooded hill country lying southeast from Sevilla, while Navarro hastened to obey the summons of the Spanish General.

"How long have you known the Señor Remelios?" was the first question asked of the young Lieutenant.

"Only since meeting him in Holguin, where General Pando introduced us, and ordered me to accompany him."

"Have you noted anything suspicious in his actions—anything that would lead you to suspect him of being other than what he claims?"

"I have not, sir," answered the Lieutenant, calmly, though with inward trepidation, since the question showed that a suspicion of some kind had been directed against his friend.

"Neither have I," said the General; "for he has admirably performed the duties assigned to him. At the same time I am desirous of asking him some questions, and so have sent for him. I will request also that you remain during our interview, and carefully compare his answers with your own knowledge of his recent movements."

Just here the Major who had recognized Ridge, and who had gone to bring him to headquarters, returned with the information that he whom they sought was not to be found.

"Do you know where he is?" asked the General, sharply, of Lieutenant Navarro.

"I do not, sir, though I think it likely that he has started for Siboney, where we had planned to go together to watch the American ships."

"Then you will accompany Major Alvarez to that place, find the Señor Remelios, and use your friendly influence to bring him back here. If for any reason he should refuse to come, he must be compelled by force, for he is suspected of being an American spy. I tell you this, because there is no question of Lieutenant Navarro's loyalty, and I assign you to this duty to show how entirely I trust you."

"I will do my best, sir," replied the young Spaniard, acknowledging this compliment with a bow. Then, wondering in which direction his duty really lay, he departed in company with the Major, who was impatient to make good his charges against the Señor Remelios.

Lieutenant Navarro had been moody and unhappy ever since the coming of the American transports. He had not confided his trouble to his companion, but had performed his duties mechanically, and would not talk of anything else. Ridge noticed this change in his friend, and had formed a shrewd guess as to its cause, but waited for the other to speak first concerning it.

In the mean time, as the young trooper neared Daiquiri, he met scouts from Captain del Rey's detachment hastening towards headquarters with news that the Americans were landing. At this he increased his speed, until he finally reached the hill agreed upon as a place of meeting with Navarro, and then his heart was thrilled with the sight outspread before him. Half a dozen transports and a few of the smaller war-ships lay in the little harbor. Steam-launches towing strings of boats crowded with troops were plying between the ships and the one small pier that offered a landing-place. The Spaniards had retreated, burning houses and bridges behind them, and already dark masses of American troops were forming on the narrow strip of level land separating the hills from the sea. These were his own people, and Ridge longed to rush forward and join them, but was faced by two obstacles. One was a strong Spanish force concealed in a ravine between him and the Americans as though to dispute their advance at that point, and the other was the memory that he had promised to await at this place the coming of Navarro, whom he expected to see with each minute.

Suddenly, as he impatiently wondered what he ought to do, there came a quick rush of feet, and the young Spaniard, breathless with haste, stood beside him.

"Amigo," he gasped, "you are in great danger. By some mischance the General has discovered that you are an American, and Major Alvarez is charged with your capture. You have been traced to this point, and even now the hill is being surrounded to prevent your escape. Within two minutes soldiers will ascend from all sides, and, until they come, you are my prisoner."

At this Ridge started back and clapped a hand to his pistol.

"But I do not forget," continued the other, "that I am also your prisoner, on parole not to fight against your countrymen, or that to you I owe my life. So I am come to save yours and aid your escape, or die beside you in making the attempt. First, though, let us exchange prisoners, for, amigo, it has come to me within these two days that I cannot desert my own people in this time of their need. Let me then remain with them until all is over, which must be shortly. Then, if I still live, I will return to you and seek my cousin. Oh, my friend, grant me this favor, and with every breath I will thank you! May it be so? Will you do as I ask?"

"Of course I will," answered Ridge, heartily. "I had already guessed your feelings, and made up my mind to give back your parole if you should ask for it. So now you are free to act as seems to you best."

"God bless you, amigo!" cried the young Spaniard, his face radiant with joy. "Now they come! Conceal yourself, while I do what may be done to save you."

## CHAPTER XXII

### ROLLO IN CUBA

THE sound of voices and of men crashing through the underbrush as they advanced up the hill from all sides was distinctly heard, and Ridge realized, with dismay, how completely he was surrounded. It did not seem possible that he could escape, but he mechanically obeyed his friend's instructions, and, diving into a dense thicket, lay flat on the ground beneath its leafy shelter.

At that same moment Navarro raised a great shout of "Here he is! There he goes! Look out for him!" He also fired several shots in rapid succession; and one of these wounding the horse that Ridge had ridden, sent it crashing in terrified flight directly towards the Spanish troops in the ravine. After the flying animal sprang the lieutenant, firing as he ran, and yelling to those on the hill to follow him.

With savage cries, and as eagerly as hounds in sight of a fox, the Spaniards gave over their careful beating of every covert, and rushed from all sides towards the scene of disturbance. Several of them passed so close to Ridge that he could have touched them, but in their blind haste they failed to notice him. In another moment they had swept over the crest of the hill and were plunging down its farther side. Before they reached the bottom, Ridge's wounded and terrified horse burst from cover directly among the ambushed troops in the ravine, by whom it was quickly killed. Then came the pursuers.

"Where is he? What have you done with him?" demanded Lieutenant Navarro, excitedly.

"Who, señor?"

"The spy! The Americano!"

"We have seen no one, only this brute of a horse."

"But he was mounted on it. I saw him and fired. He fled in this direction, and we pursued him."

"He must have been hit and fallen from the saddle."

"Then he is still close at hand," panted Major Alvarez, who had just reached the scene, "and alive or dead we must find him. Scatter, men, and search!" he added, fiercely, turning to the baffled soldiers of his command, who were crowding confusedly behind him.

This command was never obeyed; for at that moment, with a shriek and a roar, a shell from one of the American war-ships dropped into the ravine, and burst among the startled Spaniards. Their presence had been detected by the firing on the hillside, and with the range thus obtained the Yankee gunners sent shell after shell with deadly precision among the ambushed troops.

Completely demoralized by the awful effect of this fire, the Spaniards broke from cover and fled, leaving a score of dead behind, and bearing with them a desperately wounded officer. They carried him as far as Sevilla, which place they did not reach until the following morning, and where General Linares bent pityingly over him.

"Loyal and brave even unto death," he murmured. "For this last faithful service to Spain you shall rank as Captain." Then, as the closed eyes of the wounded man were opened with a look of recognition, the General turned to those who had brought him, and said:

"He is too valuable to our cause, and too brave a Spaniard to die if we can save his life. Therefore carry Captain Navarro to the hospital in Santiago, and deliver my orders that he receive the best of care."

So the painful journey was resumed, but on the crest of San Juan Heights, overlooking the city, the litter-bearers found that they were carrying a dead man. It was useless to convey him farther, and a little later they buried him, with full military honors, on the sunny slope that was shortly destined to become the scene of one of the world's decisive battles.

In the mean time Ridge Norris, snatched from the very jaws of destruction by the prompt devotion of his prisoner-friend, had emerged from his concealment, and hastened down the hill in a direction opposite to that taken by those who sought his life.

After awhile, believing that he had gained a safe distance from them, he paused to consider his situation. A minute later, when he had just planned to make a great circuit that should outflank the Spaniards in the ravine, and bring him to where the Americans were landing, a rush of approaching feet and a medley of voices caused him to plunge into the dense growth bordering the trail. Then catching a glimpse of the retreating Spaniards, whom he imagined to be searching for him, he forced his way still deeper into the tangle, until they were lost to hearing as well as to sight.

Half an hour afterwards, reassured by the unbroken silence of his surroundings, our young American attempted to regain the trail he had left, but, to his dismay, had failed to do so when darkness overtook him. The idea of spending a night in that Cuban jungle was decidedly unpleasant; but as there was nothing else to be done, Ridge quickly made such preparations for it as his limited resources would allow. His knowledge of Cuban woodcraft was much greater now than it had been two weeks earlier, and within fifteen minutes he had constructed a rude hammock of tough vines, over which was laid a great palm-leaf. This would at least swing him clear of the ground, with its pestilent dampness and swarming land-crabs. Although he knew that he should suffer from cold before morning, he dared not light a fire, for it would be almost certain to attract unwelcome attention. So he lined his swinging-bed with such dried grasses as he could find, and nestling in it tried to sleep. For hours this was impossible. The forest about him was filled with strange rattlings, clashings, and other indescribable sounds. He was also cold and hungry. But at length he lost consciousness of his unhappy position, and drifted into troubled dreams.

When next he awoke the sun was shining, and there was a confusion of voices close at hand. He could not catch the drift of conversation; but, as the tongue spoken was Spanish, he lay motionless and listened, expecting each moment to be discovered by some straggler. For several hours his unseen neighbors cooked, ate, smoked cigarettes, laughed, and talked without suspecting his presence within a few yards of them; while he, desperately hungry, cramped, and filled with impatience at this aggravating detention, wondered if they were going to stay there forever.

When, after what seemed an eternity of suspense, those who had unwittingly kept him prisoner took their departure, the sun had passed its meridian, and Ridge, parched with thirst, was suffering as much from the breathless heat as he had with cold a few hours earlier. As he cautiously approached the scene of the recent bivouac he found it to be where a small stream crossed a narrow trail, and, after quenching his thirst, he followed the latter in what he believed to be the direction of Daiquiri. At any rate, it was the opposite one from that taken by his recent unwelcome neighbors. Up hill and down the dim trail led him, across streams and through dark ravines, but always buried in dense foliage, through which he could gain no outlook.

After our young trooper had followed the devious course of this rough pathway for several miles, he suddenly came to a halt, and stood spellbound. From directly ahead of him came a burst of music swelling grandly through the solemn stillness of the forest. A regimental band was playing "The Star-spangled Banner," and never before had such glorious notes been borne to his ears. Tears started to his eyes; but without pausing to brush them away he dashed forward. A minute later he stood on the brow of a declivity looking down upon the sea-coast village of Siboney, which he instantly recognized, though its transformation from what it was when he had last seen it was wonderful. Then it had been a stronghold of Spanish troops. Now the fortifications crowning its encircling hills, abandoned by those who had erected them, stood empty and harmless; while in the village, and on the narrow plain surrounding it, an advance-guard of the American army was pitching its tents. Over a building on a hill-side opposite to where Ridge stood, which he remembered as headquarters of the Spanish Commandant, floated an American flag, evidently just raised, and from that quarter also came the inspiring music that had so quickened his pulses.

Ten minutes later he stood before that very building, having passed through the American lines unquestioned, though stared at curiously by those who noticed him at all. He wore the first Spanish uniform they had ever seen, and, not recognizing it, they took him for a Cuban officer, several of whom had already visited the camp. So the young American, looking in vain for a familiar face among the thousand or so of his busy countrymen, made his way to headquarters, where, for the first time, a sentry halted him and demanded his business.

While he was thus detained an officer issued from the building, mounted a horse, and was about to ride away when Ridge sprang forward, calling:

"General! General Lawton!"

The officer halted, looked keenly at the sun-browned young man in Spanish uniform, and, almost without hesitation, said:

"You are Sergeant Norris of the Rough Riders, I believe?"

"Yes, sir," replied Ridge, saluting, and overjoyed at being recognized.

"I looked for you at Daiquiri," continued the General, "and hope you can give good reason for not reporting there as ordered."

"I believe I can, sir."

"Then come in with me and give it to Major-General Wheeler, who is at present in command."

Within half an hour the young scout had been complimented by both Generals on the success of his recent undertaking, and had furnished them with information of the utmost value concerning the obstacles to be encountered between Siboney and Santiago. The first of these he stated would be found at Las Guasimas, where the two trails from Siboney to Sevilla on the Santiago road formed a junction some three miles inland. A little later he had the honor of guiding General Wheeler on a reconnoissance over one of these trails, and pointing out the location of a strongly intrenched Spanish force, posted to oppose the American advance.

When they returned to Siboney the sun had set, and Ridge, faint for the want of food, was wondering where he should find a supper, when a mighty cheering, mingled with wild cowboy yells, rose from a point where the Daiquiri road entered the village.

"It sounds as though your irrepressible comrades had arrived," said the little General, turning to his young guide with a quizzical smile, "though I did not expect them before to-morrow. Perhaps you would like to go and welcome them."

"Thank you, sir. Indeed I should," and in another moment Ridge was hastening in the direction of the familiar sounds.

How his heart swelled with loving pride, as he sighted the red and white guidons of the on-sweeping column; and when the one bearing the magical letter "K" came into view, he could have wept for very joy.

But he didn't weep. There wasn't any time, for in another minute he was among them, proclaiming his identity to incredulous ears.

When the Riders of Troop K were finally forced to acknowledge that he was really their own sergeant whom they believed was left behind in Tampa, all military discipline was for the moment flung to the winds. They yelled and whooped and danced about him, slapping him on the back, wringing his hands, and acting so like madmen, that the rest of the command stared at them in blank amazement.

As for Rollo Van Kyp, he first hugged his recovered tent-mate into breathlessness, and then invited the entire troop to take supper with him at the Waldorf in celebration of the prodigal Sergeant's return. To this invitation a hundred voices answered as one:

"Yes, we will! Yes, we will! Rollo in Cuba, yes, we will!"

## CHAPTER XXIII

### THE "TERRORS" IN BATTLE

"COULDN'T you let me begin that supper with a hardtack right now?" pleaded our hungry young trooper, as soon as he could make himself heard. "It's a day and a half since my last meal, which was only a small ration of boiled rice, and it seems as though a hardtack at this minute would do me more good than the promise of a hundred Waldorf suppers."

The hunger that demanded even a despised hardtack was at that time so incredible to the well-fed Riders, that at first they could not believe his request to be made in earnest. When, however, they saw the eagerness with which he began to devour one of the iron-clad biscuits, hesitatingly offered by Rollo Van Kyp, they were convinced that he was indeed on the verge of starvation. They were also reminded of their own keen appetites, for, amid the excitement of that day's landing and their forced march from Daiquiri, they had eaten nothing since a daylight breakfast. But each man carried three days' rations, and camp-fires were quickly ablaze in every direction. From these delicious odors of boiling coffee and frizzling bacon so stimulated their hunger, that when, tin cup and plate in hand, they sat down to that first meal on Cuban soil, they pronounced it equal to any ever served in New York City.

While Ridge, sharing his chum's cup and plate, was striving between mouthfuls of this thoroughly enjoyable supper to answer a few of the innumerable questions showered upon him, he suddenly became aware of an officer standing on the edge of the fire-light and regarding him with interest. As our young trooper sprang to his feet with a salute, he was covered with confusion to recognize in the motionless figure his own Lieutenant-Colonel, and to remember that in all this time he had neglected to report his return to the regiment. He began a confused apology, but the other interrupted him, laughing.

"It is all right, Sergeant," he said. "We heard of you from General Wheeler, who, by-the-way, is much pleased with the results of your expedition. So I came to find you, with a reprimand for not having reported at once to Colonel Wood, but when I saw you devouring hardtack, I was quite willing to accept starvation as your excuse. Now, however, the Colonel would be pleased to see you."

After an hour spent at headquarters, where he was honored with an invitation to eat a second supper, during which his apparently unappeasable appetite for hardtack and bacon caused much amusement, Ridge was allowed to return to his comrades. A throng of these gathered about the camp-fire of Rollo Van Kyp's mess, and, unmindful of the showers that fell at short intervals, listened for hours with breathless interest and undisguised envy to the story of his recent adventures. They were happily reassured by his description of the strength of Santiago's fortifications, and his assertion that the Spaniards would put up a good fight before surrendering them ; for they had been inclined to think and speak contemptuously of the enemy who they feared would yield without a struggle.

So the greater part of the night was passed. They ought to have been asleep, storing up strength against the morrow ; but who could sleep amid the uproar and excitement of that first night at Siboney? Not the Rough Riders, at any rate. Half a dozen transports had come into the little bay ; and from them scores of boat-loads of troops and supplies were being landed through the roaring surf on the open beach. A thousand naked figures, screaming, ducking, and splashing one another like so many schoolboys on a frolic, assisted and impeded the landing of their comrades, who, crowded into pontoons and small boats, were pitched, howling with delight, from the crest of each in-rolling breaker. A half-moon and the powerful search-lights of two war-ships flooded the whole extraordinary scene with brightness. On shore the dripping arrivals crowded about the red camp-fires drying their soaking uniforms, cooking, eating, singing, laughing, and filled with irrepressible happiness at having escaped from their "prison hulks" and reached Cuba at last.

Thus, at dead of night, was an army landed on a hostile shore, and by two o'clock in the morning five thousand American troops were crowded in and about the village of Siboney.

Acting on the reports brought him by Ridge Norris and by certain Cubans whom the Spanish rearguard had driven back the day before, as well as upon the knowledge gained by his own reconnoissance, General Wheeler had determined to attack the enemy, who were strongly posted at the forking of two roads leading from Siboney to Sevilla. The broader of these roads bore to the right through a narrow valley, while the other, merely a rough trail, climbed the hill back of the village and followed the crest of a ridge to the place of intersection. Both passed through an almost impenetrable growth of small trees and underbrush, thickly set with palms, bamboos, Spanish-bayonets, thorn bushes, and cactus, all bound together by a tangle of tough vines, and interspersed with little glades of rank grasses. To the right-hand trail, miscalled the wagon-road, were assigned eight troops from two regiments of dismounted regular cavalry, the First and Tenth (colored), under General Young. With these Colonel Wood and his Rough Riders, advancing over the hill-trail, were to form a junction at the forks, locally known as Las Guasimas, three miles away.

So at earliest dawn the troops detailed for this

duty were astir, after but three hours of troubled sleep. The regulars, having the longer route to traverse, were given a half-hour's start of the others, who, in the mean time, made coffee and bolted a few mouthfuls of food. Then troops were formed, First Sergeants called the roll, the order, "Forward march!" was given, and the Riders, burdened with blanket-rolls, haversacks, canteens, tin cups, carbines, and cartridge-belts filled to their utmost capacity, began to scramble up the steep hill-side.

The sun was already red and hot, the steaming air was breathless, and by the time the top of the first hill was gained the panting troopers were bathed in perspiration that trickled from them in rivulets. A short breathing-space was allowed, and then, with Ridge Norris and a Cuban scout to feel the way, the line of march was again taken up. Next behind the scouts came a "point" of five men, then Capron's troop strung out in single file and acting as advance-guard. Behind these followed the main body of the little army, headed by Colonel Wood. For an hour and a half they toiled forward in this fashion, laughing, joking, commenting on the tropical strangeness of their surroundings, and wondering if there was a Spaniard nearer to them than Santiago.

At length a halt was called, and the wearied men, suffering greatly from the sweltering heat, gladly flung themselves to the ground. At the same moment Ridge was reporting to Colonel Wood that he had located the Spaniards only a few hundred yards ahead, and behind strong intrenchments. Upon this the Colonel moved cautiously forward to study the position, leaving his men to fan themselves with their hats and exchange laughing comments upon one another's appearance, utterly unconscious of the enemy's proximity.

Suddenly word was passed back for silence in the ranks. Then came "Attention!" and "Load carbines!"

"Something must be up," whispered Rollo Van Kyp to Mark Gridley, and just then all eyes were directed inquiringly towards Ridge Norris, who was taking a place with his own troop.

"The Spaniards are right in front of us," he whispered, and almost instantly the startling news was passed down the line. There was no joking now, nor complaints of the heat, but each man stood with compressed lips, peering into the dense underbrush on either side, and wishing that the suspense was over.

Now came the hurried forming of a line of battle. One troop was sent straight to the front, two were deployed to the left, and two more, one of which was that of Ridge and Rollo, were ordered to force their way through the thickets on their right, down into the valley, where they were to make connection with the regulars. While these movements were being executed, and with a suddenness that caused every man's nerves to tingle, a sharp firing began somewhere off in the right, and ran like a flash of powder along the whole line.

Blanket-rolls and haversacks had already been flung aside, and the sweating troopers, with their flannel shirts open at the throat and sleeves rolled up to the elbows, bore only their carbines, ammunition, and canteens of water. At first Ridge had only his revolver, but within five minutes he had snatched up the carbine of a man who fell dead at his side, and was as well armed as the rest.

For an hour the Riders fought blindly, seeing no enemy, but pouring their own volleys in the direction from which the steady streams of Mauser bullets seemed to come. The smokeless powder used by the Spaniards gave no trace of their location, while the sulphurous cloud hanging over the Americans formed a perfect target for the Spanish fire.

Still the dark-blue line was steadily advanced, sometimes by quick rushes, and again by a crawling on hands and knees through the high, hot grass. Always over the heads of the troopers and among them streamed a ceaseless hail of bullets from Mauser rifles and machine-guns. Men fell with each minute, some not to rise again, some only wounded; but the others never paused to note their fate. Those who could must push on and get at the Spaniards. Those who were helpless to advance must, for the present, be left to care for themselves as best they might.

At length the ever-advancing line reached the edge of a grassy valley set here and there with clumps of palms. To the left was a stone building, formerly a distillery, now a Spanish fort, and directly in front was an intrenched ridge. To this the Spaniards had been slowly but surely driven, and now they occupied their strongest position.

At almost the same moment, and as though animated by a single thought, Roosevelt on the extreme left and Wood on the right gave the order to charge. With a yell the panting, smoke-begrimed Riders broke from cover and sprang after their dauntless leaders. They charged by rushes, running fifty feet, then dropping in the hot grass and firing; then reload, rise, and run forward. On their right the regulars were doing the same thing in the same manner with the precision of machines, while the colored troops stormed the ridge with a steadiness and grim determination that won for them undying fame, and answered forever the question as to whether or not the negro is fitted to be a soldier.

The assault was unsupported by artillery; those making it had no bayonets, and the Spanish fire, ripping, crackling, and blazing in vivid sheets from block-house and rifle-pit, was doubling and trebling in fury; but there was no hesitation on the part of the Americans, no backward step.

The Spaniards could not understand it. This thin line of yelling men advancing with such confidence must have the whole American army close behind them. In that case another minute would see an assault by overwhelming numbers. Thus thinking, the Spaniards faltered, glanced uneasily behind them, and finally ran, panic-stricken, towards Santiago, while Rough Riders and regulars swarmed with exulting yells and howls of triumph into the abandoned trenches. The first land battle of the war had been fought and won. Wood, Roosevelt, Young, Rough Riders, and regulars had covered themselves with glory, and performed a deed of heroism that will never be forgotten so long as the story of the American soldier is told.

"If we only had our horses we could catch every one of those chaps," said Rollo Van Kyp, as he sat in a window of the ruined building just captured by the Riders, happily swinging his legs and fanning himself with his hat. The young millionaire's face was black with powder, covered with blood from the scratching of thorns, and streaked with trickling perspiration. His shirt and trousers were in rags.

"It's a beastly shame we weren't allowed to bring them," he continued, "for this fighting on foot in the tropics is disgustingly hot work. Now if I were in Teddy's place—"

"Private Van Kyp," interrupted Sergeant Norris, sternly, "instead of criticising your superiors you had better go and wash your face, for your personal appearance is a disgrace to the troop. But oh, Rollo!" he added, unable longer to maintain the assumed dignity under which he had tried to hide his exultation, "wasn't it a bully fight? and aren't you glad we're here? and don't you wish the home folks could see us at this very minute?"

## CHAPTER XXIV

### FACING SAN JUAN HEIGHTS

THE fight of Las Guasimas, in which Rough Riders and colored regulars covered themselves with glory, was only a first brisk skirmish between the advanced outposts of opposing armies, but its influence on both sides was equal to that of a pitched battle. It furnished a notable example of the steadiness and bull-dog tenacity of the American regular, as well as the absolute fearlessness and determination to win, at any cost, of the dudes and cowboys banded under the name of Rough Riders. It afforded striking proof that it is not the guns, but the men behind them, who win battles, since an inferior force, unsupported by artillery, and unprovided with bayonets, had charged and driven from strong intrenchments nearly four times their own number of an enemy armed with vastly superior weapons. It inspired the Americans with confidence in themselves and their leaders, while it weakened that of the Spaniards in both. To the Rough Riders it was a glorious and splendidly won victory, and as they swarmed over the intrenchments, from which the fire of death had been so fiercely hurled at them that morning, they yelled themselves hoarse with jubilant cheers.

Then came the reaction. They were exhausted with the strain of excitement and their tremendous exertions under the pitiless tropical sun. Strong men who had fought with tireless energy all at once found themselves trembling with weakness, and the entire command welcomed the order to make camp on the grassy banks of a clear stream shaded by great trees.

In their baptism of fire eight of the Riders had been killed outright, thirty-four more were seriously wounded, and fully half of the remainder could show the scars of grazing bullets or tiny clean-cut holes through their clothing, telling of escapes from death by the fraction of an inch. Ridge Norris, for instance, found a livid welt across his chest, looking as though traced by a live coal, and marking the course of a bullet that, with a hair's deflection, would have ended his life, while Rollo Van Kyp's hat seemed to have been an especial target for Spanish rifles.

After regaining their breath, and receiving assurance that the enemy had retreated beyond their present reach, these two, in company with many others, went back over the battle-field to look up the wounded, and bring forward the packs flung aside at the beginning of the fight.

At sunset that evening the Riders buried their dead, in a long single grave lined with palm-leaves, on a breezy hill-side overlooking the scene of their victory. The laying to rest of these comrades, who, only a few hours before, had been so full of life with all its hopes and ambitions, was the most impressive ceremony in which any of the survivors had ever engaged. It strengthened their loyalty and devotion to each other and to their cause as nothing else could have done, and as the entire command gathered close about the open grave to sing "Nearer my God to Thee," many a voice was choked with feelings too solemn for expression, and many a suntanned cheek was wet with tears. The camp of the Rough Riders was very quiet that night, and the events of the day just closed were discussed in low tones, as though in fear of awakening the sleepers on the near-by hill-side.

After the fight of Las Guasimas, its heroes rested and waited for six days, while the remainder of the army effected its landing and made its slow way to the position they had won over the narrow trails they had cleared. These days of waiting were also days of vast discomfort, and the patient endurance of drenching tropical rains and steaming heat, the wearing of the same battle-soiled clothing day after day and night after night, and, above all, of an ever-present hunger, that sapped both strength and spirits. They had started out with but three days' rations, and four days passed before a scanty supply of hard-tack, bacon, and coffee began to dribble into camp. The road to Siboney, flooded by constant rains, bowlder-strewn, and inches deep in mud, was for a long time impassable to wagons; and during those six days such supplies of food and ammunition as reached the idle army were brought to it by three trains of pack-mules that toiled ceaselessly back and forth between the coast and the front, bringing the barest necessities of life, but nothing more.

So the American army suffered and prayed to be led forward, while the Spaniards between them and Santiago strengthened their own position with every hour, and confidently awaited their coming. The invaders now occupied the Sevilla plateau, and were within five miles of the city they sought to capture. In their front lay a broad wooded valley, to them an unknown region, and on its farther side rose a range of hills, that Ridge Norris told them were the San Juan Heights, strongly protected by block-houses, rifle-pits, and bewildering entanglements of barbed wire, a feature of modern warfare now appearing for the first time in history. With their glasses, from the commanding eminence of El Poso Hill, crowned with the ruined buildings of an abandoned plantation, the American officers could distinctly see the Spaniards at work on their intrenchments a mile and a half away, and note the ever-lengthening lines of freshly excavated earth.

But for six days the army waited, and its artillery, which was expected to seriously impair, if not utterly destroy the effectiveness of those ever-growing earthworks, still reposed peacefully on board the ships that had brought it to Cuba. Only two light batteries had been landed, and on the sixth day after Las Guasimas these reached the front. At the same time came word that General Pando with 5000 Spanish reinforcements was nearing the besieged city from the north. In that direction, and only three miles from Santiago, lay the fortified village of Caney, held by a strong force of Spanish troops. If it were captured, Pando's advance might be cut off. So General Shafter, coming ashore for the first time a week after the landing of his troops, planned a forward movement with this object in view. Lawton's division was to capture Caney, and then swing round so as to sever all outside communication with Santiago. While he was doing this, demonstrations that should deter the Spaniards from sending an additional force in that direction were to be made against San Juan and Aguadores. These movements were to occupy one day, and on the next the reunited army was to attack the entire line of the San Juan ridge. In the mean time no one knew anything of the valley lying between this strongly protected ridge and those who proposed to capture it.

So the order was issued, and late in the afternoon of June 30th, in a pouring rain, the camps were broken, and the drenched army eagerly began its forward movement. Lawton's division marching off to the right slipped and stumbled through the mud along a narrow, almost impassable, trail over the densely wooded hills until eight o'clock that evening, when, within a mile of Caney, it lay down for the night in the wet grass without tents or fire, and amid a silence strictly enjoined, for fear lest the

Spaniards should discover its presence, and run away before morning.

At the same time Wheeler's division of dismounted cavalry, including the Rough Riders and Kent's infantry division, advanced as best it could over the horrible Santiago road, ankle-deep in mud and water, to El Poso Hill, on and about which it passed a wretchedly uncomfortable night. Seven thousand heavily equipped men, mingled with horses, artillery, pack-mules, and army wagons, all huddled into a narrow gully slippery with mud, advance so slowly, however eager they may be to push forward, that although the movement was begun at four o'clock, midnight found the rearmost regiment still plodding wearily forward.

With the coming of daylight, on July 1st, the army lay beneath a dense blanket of mist that spread its wet folds over the entire region they were to traverse. It was eight o'clock before Grimes's battery of four light field-pieces, posted on El Poso Hill, opened an ineffective fire upon the heights across the broad valley. For twenty minutes the Spaniards paid no attention to the harmless barking of the little guns; then the smoke cloud hanging over them proved so admirable and attractive a target that they could no longer resist firing at it. So shells began to fall about the battery with such startling accuracy that a score of Americans and Cubans gathered near it were killed or wounded before they could seek shelter. Among these first victims of the San Juan fight were several of the Rough Riders.

About this time General Sumner, temporarily in command of the cavalry, was ordered to advance his troops into the valley as far as the edge of the wooded belt, and within half a mile of the San Juan batteries.

"What shall I do when I get there?" asked General Sumner.

"Await further orders," was the curt reply.

There were other changes in commands that morning; for Brigadier-General Young, being prostrated by a fever, the Colonel of the Rough Riders was assigned to his duties, and became "General" Wood from that hour. At the same time his Lieutenant-Colonel stepped into the vacancy thus created, and as "Colonel" Roosevelt was destined to win for himself and his dashing command immortal fame before the setting of that day's sun.

So the Rough Riders, together with five other regiments of dismounted cavalry, started down the deep-cut road, which in places was not over ten feet wide, and was everywhere sticky with mud, while an entire infantry division was crowded into it behind them. Like all other roads in that country, this one, now densely packed with human beings advancing at a snail's pace along nearly three miles of its length, was bordered on both sides by an impenetrable tropical jungle.

The Spaniards were advised of the forward movement, and though they could not see it, were already directing a hot fire at this road, of whose location they were, of course, well aware, and from the outset dead and wounded men marked the line of American progress. After a mile of marching under these conditions, the foremost troops came to a place where the San Juan River crossed the road. A short distance beyond it crossed again, thus forming the ox-bow to be known ever after that memorable day as the "Bloody Bend." A little farther on was open country, and here General Sumner obeyed instructions by deploying his troopers to the right in a long skirmish line on the edge of the timber. In this position they lay down, sheltering themselves as best they could behind bushes or in the tall hot grass, and anxiously awaited further orders from headquarters. The Spanish fire, which they might not return, was ceaseless and pitiless, though because of absence of smoke none could see whence it came.

Already the loss in killed and wounded was assuming alarming proportions, and still on-coming troops were pouring into that Bloody Bend, where they must accept, with what fortitude they could command, their awful baptism of fire. Fifty feet above their heads floated the observation balloon of the engineers, betraying their exact position and forming an admirable focus for the enemy's fire, which, after awhile, to the vast relief of every one, shot the balloon to pieces so that it dropped from sight among the trees.

For hours the troops waited thus in the frightful tropical heat, monuments of patient endurance. The dead and the living lay side by side, though such of the wounded as could be reached were dragged back to dressing-stations on the riverbanks. Even here they were not safe, for the dense foliage that afforded a grateful shade also concealed scores of Spanish sharp-shooters. These maintained a cowardly and deadly fire, the source of which could rarely be discovered, upon all coming within range, regardless of whether they were wounded men, surgeons in discharge of their duties, hospital stewards, or Red Cross assistants, thus adding a fresh horror to warfare.

It was a terrible position, and the American army was being cut to pieces without a chance to fire a gun in self-defence. To advance appeared suicidal, to attempt a retreat meant utter destruction. No orders could come over the blockaded road from the Commander-in-Chief, miles in the rear, nor could word of the awful situation be sent back to him in time. The men thus trapped gazed at one another with the desperate look of hunted animals brought to bay. Must they all die, and was there no salvation?

Suddenly a mounted officer dashed into the open, pointing with his sword to the nearest hill crowned by a block-house. Then through a storm of bullets he spurred towards it, and, with a mighty yell ringing high above the crash of battle, his men sprang after him.

## CHAPTER XXV

### RIDGE WINS HIS SWORD

A FEW minutes before this, while the Rough Riders lay in sullen despair, with death on all sides and filling the air above them, a staff-officer from headquarters, keenly anxious concerning the situation and for the honor of his chief, appeared among them. Whatever happened, he could not afford to betray uneasiness or fear. So he walked erect as calmly as though inspecting troops on parade, apparently unconscious of the bullets that buzzed like hornets about him. He was studying the position of the several regiments, and his face lighted with a smile as he found himself among the men of the First Volunteer Cavalry.

"Hello, Rough Riders!" he cried. "Glad to see you taking things so cool and comfortable. By-the-way, there is a promotion for one of you waiting at headquarters. It came by cable last evening. Sergeant Norris is promoted to a lieutenancy for distinguished service. If any one knows where he is, let the word be passed. It may be an encouragement for him to hear the good-news."

Those men near enough to catch the officer's

words raised a cheer, and Ridge, who lay among them, sprang to his feet with a flushed face.

"That's him!" shouted Rollo Van Kyp, and the officer, stepping forward with extended hand, said, "I congratulate you, Lieutenant Norris, and am proud to make your acquaintance."

At that moment Colonel Roosevelt, on horseback, and so forming the most conspicuous target for Spanish bullets on the whole field, dashed to the front, pointed to the nearest block-house, and called upon his men to follow him. With a yell they sprang forward, and Ridge, being already on his feet, raced with the front rank.

In line with the Rough Riders were their fighting partners, the black riders of the Tenth United States Cavalry, and at the first intimation of an advance these leaped forward in eager rivalry of their white comrades. Across the plain they charged, and then up the steep hill-side, while the Spanish fire doubled in fury, and the tall grass in front of them was cut as though by the scythe of a mower. Spectators in the rear gazed appalled at the thin line of troopers thus rushing to what seemed certain destruction.

"It is not war—it is suicide!" cried a foreign attaché.

Whatever it was, it afforded an example that others were quick to follow, and the moment the intention of the Rough Riders became evident, regiment after regiment on the left—dismounted cavalry and infantry, regulars and volunteers, Hawkins's men and Kent's—broke from the cover that had afforded them so little protection, and swept across the open towards the deadly intrenchments crowning the main ridge of San Juan Heights. There was no order for this glorious charge. The commanding generals had not even contemplated such a bit of splendid but reckless daring. Even now, so hopeless did it seem, they would have stopped it if they could; but they might as well have tried to arrest the rush of an avalanche by wishing. It was a voluntary movement of men goaded beyond further endurance by suffering and suspense. As one of the foreign military spectators afterwards said, "It was a grand popular uprising, and, like most such, it proved successful."

The Rough Riders and the negro troopers who charged with them had no bayonets, and did but little firing until more than half-way up the hill they had undertaken to capture. With carbines held across their breasts, they simply moved steadily forward without a halt or a backward glance. Behind them the slope was dotted with their dead and wounded, but the survivors took no heed of their depleted ranks. Roosevelt, with the silken cavalry banner fluttering beside him, led the way, and there was no man who would not follow him to the death.

Half-way up the hill-side Ridge Norris pitched headlong to the ground, and some one said: "Poor fellow! News of his promotion came just in time." As the young Lieutenant fell, another officer, cheering on his men immediately behind him, also dropped, pierced with bullets. The sword that he had been waving was flung far in advance, and as Ridge, who had only stumbled over an unnoticed mound of earth, regained his feet unharmed, he saw it lying in front of him and picked it up. He was entitled to carry a sword now, and here was one to his hand.

The Spaniards could not believe that these few men, frantically climbing that bullet-swept hill-side, would ever gain the crest. So they doggedly held their position, firing with the regularity of machines, and expecting with each moment to see the American ranks melt away or break in precipitate flight. They did melt away in part, but not wholly, and their only flight was a very slow one that bore them steadily upward.

Just under the brow of the hill they paused for a long breath, and then leaped forward in a fierce final rush. Over the rifle-pits they poured, tearing down the barbed-wire barricades with their bare hands, and making a dash for the block-house. Already the dismayed Spaniards were streaming down the farther side of the hill. A last withering volley crashed from the loop-holed building, and then its defenders also took to panic-stricken flight. In another minute the flaunting banner of Spain had been torn down, and the stars and stripes of freedom waved proudly in its place. At the same moment, from earthwork and rifle-pit fluttered the yellow silk flags of the cavalry and the troop guidons; while to distant ears the news of victory was borne by the cheer of exhausted but intensely happy men.

Many of them were for the moment incapable of further effort, but as many more, inspired with fresh strength by success, dashed down the opposite side of the hill in pursuit of the flying Spaniards. Among these was Ridge Norris, waving his newly acquired sword, and yelling that there were other hills yet to be captured. A few minutes later these found themselves madly charging, for a second time, up a steep, bullet-swept slope in company with other cavalrymen and long lines of infantry. Now they were assaulting San Juan Heights, defended by the strongest line of works outside of Santiago. The Spaniards had deemed the position impregnable, and so it would have been to any troops on earth save Americans or British ; but the men now swarming up its slippery front not only believed it could be taken, but that they could take it. And they did take it, as the first hill had been taken, by sheer pluck and dauntless determination. In vain did the Spaniards hurl forth their deadliest fire of machine-gun and rifle. The grim American advance was as unchecked as that of an ocean tide. Finally it surged with a roar like that of a storm-driven breaker over the crest, and dashed with resistless fury against the crowning fortifications. In another minute the Spaniards were in full flight, and from the hard-won heights of San Juan thousands of panting, cheering, jubilant Yankee soldiers were gazing for the first time upon the city of Santiago, which, only three miles away, lay at their feet, and apparently at their mercy.

While the troops who had thus stormed and carried San Juan were exulting over their almost incredible victory, word came that Lawton's men had performed a similar feat at Caney, and after hours of ineffective firing had finally won the forts by direct and unsupported assault.

Thus the entire line of Santiago's outer defences, many miles in length, had fallen to the Americans; but could they hold them until the arrival of their artillery? This was the question anxiously discussed at headquarters, where several of the Generals declared immediate retreat to be the only present salvation of the American army. The existing fortifications of San Juan Heights were unavailable for use against the Spaniards, and it did not seem possible that the tired troops could dig new ones in time. The enemy had as yet suffered but slight losses, and still occupied his inner line of forts, block-houses, and rifle-pits, nearly, if not quite, as strong as those just won from him. Beyond lay Santiago, with barricaded streets, loop-holed walls, and everywhere bewildering mazes of barbed wire.

While the commanding officers discussed the situation, arguing hotly for and against retreat, their men dug trenches along the farther crest of the San Juan hills. All night long they worked by the light of a full moon, excavating the gravelly soil with bayonet and meat-tin, filling hundreds of bags with sand, and laying them in front of the shallow pits, with little spaces between them, through which rifle-barrels might be thrust. At the same time they scooped out terraces on the slope up which they had charged, and there pitched their camps, a long way from drinking-water, but close to the firing-line. Thus by daylight they were ready for any movement the enemy might make. Nor were they prepared any too quickly, for with earliest dawn the Spaniards opened a heavy fire, both artillery and rifle, on the American position. In places the opposing lines were not three hundred yards apart, and across this narrow space the Spanish fire was poured with unremitting fury for fourteen consecutive hours.

The Americans only returned this fire by an occasional rifle-shot, to show that they were still on hand, and through the interminable hours of that blistering day they simply clung by sheer grit to the heights they had won.

On the previous day the Americans had lost over a thousand men killed or wounded, and during the present one-sided fight one hundred and seven more fell victims to Spanish bullets; but the trenches had been held, and that day's work settled forever the question of their retention.

In the mean time Lieutenant Norris, who had miraculously escaped unhurt from the very front of two fierce charges, was curious to know whose sword he was carrying; and so, after San Juan Heights had been safely won, he strolled back over the battle-field to try and discover its owner. After a long search he found the little mound of earth over which he had stumbled, and was startled to see it was a recently made grave. Beside it lay an officer in Rough Rider uniform, face down, and wearing an empty scabbard. His, then, was the sword; but who was he? A gentle turning of the still body revealed the placidly handsome features of the young New-Mexican, Arthur Navarro. Near the grave, across which one of his arms had been flung, as though lovingly, lay a wooden cross bearing a rudely cut inscription in Spanish. It had evidently been overthrown by the charging Americans. Now Ridge picked it up, read the inscription, and stared incredulous. "Captain Ramon Navarro, Royal Spanish Guards. Died for his country, June 22, 1898."

"My friend Ramon, killed the very day he saved me from capture!" murmured Ridge. "But how marvellous that they should have buried him here, that his grave should have saved my life by giving me that fall, and that the bullets intended for me should have taken the life of the cousin who was to have been his partner!"

So the two, one from the New World and one from the Old, who loved each other, but had been separated during life by the calls of duty, were united in death; for they buried the young New-Mexican close beside his Spanish cousin, and the grasses of San Juan Hill wave above them both.

Wearing the sword thus intrusted to him, and which he would send to far-away New Mexico at the earliest opportunity, Lieutenant Norris bore his full share of the second day's fighting on San Juan Heights. Late that night, as he was coming in from the trenches, he was called to General Sumner's tent to act as interpreter. A deserter, apparently a Spanish sailor, had just been brought in, and was evidently trying to convey some important information that no one present could understand.

"He says," exclaimed Ridge, after listening intently to the man, "that Admiral Cervera's ships—coaled, provisioned, and under full head of steam—are about to make a dash from the harbor. He thinks they will start soon after sunrise, or when our ships have drawn off to their accustomed daytime distance."

Although the reliability of this startling news was very doubtful, it was deemed of sufficient importance to be immediately transmitted to Admiral Sampson.

"Who is the best rider in your command?" asked the General, turning to Colonel Roosevelt, who had assisted at the examination of the Spanish deserter.

"Lieutenant Norris," was the unhesitating answer.

"Then let Mr. Norris take my orderly's horse, make his way with all speed to Siboney, press into service the first steam craft he comes across, and carry this fellow's statement, with my compliments, to Admiral Sampson."

Five minutes later our young trooper, once more on horseback, and in a blaze of excitement, was galloping for dear life over the rugged road by which the army had come from the coast.

## CHAPTER XXVI

#### MUTINY ON A TRANSPORT

ON the memorable morning of July 3d the sun had risen from the fog-bank that promised a hot day before our young trooper, wearied and mud-bespattered with his journey, and his face still powder-grimed with the smoke of the day's fighting, rode into the village of Siboney. It no longer presented the scenes of excited bustle and eager enthusiasm that had marked it on the eve of Las Guasimas, for the army had departed long since, and only its shattered wrecks of humanity had drifted back. Now Siboney was a place of suffering and death; for here had been established the hospitals to which wounded men limped painfully from the distant front, or were brought in heavily jolting army wagons.

On this peaceful Sunday morning—for it was Sunday, though Ridge did not know it at the time—a great stillness brooded over Siboney, and almost the only persons visible were medical attendants, who moved quietly about the big hospital tents or the fever-infested buildings that had been pressed into the same service.

In the little harbor lay but a single steam-vessel, a transport, though others could be dimly seen far out at sea, where they spent most of their time, which fact largely accounted for the woful lack of supplies at the front. A boat from the single ship that had ventured into the harbor lay on the beach discharging freight. To it Ridge hurried, and, addressing himself to the man who appeared to be in charge, said:

"I have an important communication for the Captain of your ship. Will you take me off to her?"

With a contemptuous glance at the disreputable-looking young trooper, the man answered:

"See about it when I get ready to go."

"Please make haste, then, for my business is very important, and I am in a great hurry."

"Oh, you be. Reckon you'd better swim out, then, for I've been hurried by you landlubbers 'bout as much as I propose to be on this v'y'ge."

Ridge's face flushed, and he wanted to make an angry retort; but there was no other boat available, and he could not afford to throw away this chance. So he bit his lips and silently watched the deliberate movements of the men, who seemed to find a pleasure in aggravating him by their slowness.

The boat could have been unloaded in five minutes, but the operation was made to consume a half-hour, during which time Ridge stood silent, though with finger-nails digging into the palms of his clinched hands. All at once, without a word of warning, the boat's crew began to shove their craft from the beach.

"Hold on!" cried Ridge, springing forward. "I am going with you."

"Why aren't you aboard, then?" asked the mate, with a grin, as his men gave another shove that launched the boat into deep water.

Leaping into the sea, Ridge barely succeeded in clutching a gunwale and pulling himself aboard, amid chuckles of laughter from the crew. His ducking had not improved his personal appearance, and as he now sat in the bow of the boat dripping water from every point, he formed an object for so much rude wit and coarse merriment, that upon reaching the transport he was furious with pent-up wrath.

On gaining the deck of the ship he hurried forward, and found her Captain smoking an after-breakfast cigar in his comfortably appointed cabin.

"Well, sir, who are you? and what do you want?" demanded this individual, as Ridge presented himself at the door.

"I am an army officer bearing a message of the utmost importance from General Sumner to Admiral Sampson; and as this is the only steam-vessel in the harbor, I have come to ask that you will carry me to the flag-ship."

"If you haven't got cheek!" ejaculated the Captain. "So you are an army officer, are you?"

"That is what I said."

"You don't look it. Are you the Quartermaster-General?"

"Certainly not."

"Thought not. Didn't know but what you'd claim to be, though, since he's the only army officer that I take orders from."

"But I am not giving an order. I am making a request that any American should be glad to grant, seeing that my message concerns the safety of the United States fleet, and may alter the whole course of the war."

"What is it?" demanded the Captain, bluntly.

"You have no business to ask," replied Ridge. "At the same time I will tell you, that you may be induced to get your ship under way the more quickly. The Spanish squadron is about to make a dash from Santiago Harbor with the hope of taking our fleet by surprise and escaping."

"What is that to me?" asked the Captain, coolly.

"What is that to you!" cried Ridge. "Why, some of our ships may be destroyed if they are not warned in time."

"That is their lookout, not mine. Besides, Uncle Sam can afford to pay for them; while if this ship should be injured the loss would fall on the owners, and I should lose my job."

"Do you mean that you refuse to take me out to the flag-ship?"

"Of course I do," responded the Captain; "and not one foot nearer to it, or to any other warship, does my vessel move this day than she is at present."

"Then, sir," said Ridge, still struggling to main

tain his calmness, " I will thank you to set me ashore again, as speedily as possible."

"Why should I set you ashore?" asked the Captain, with exasperating indifference. "You came on board without an invitation, and now you may stay here until the next boat is ready to run in, which will be in the course of an hour or two."

"By which time half the American fleet may have been destroyed for lack of warning," groaned Ridge. Then he added, his face blazing with anger : " I hope you are not an American, and I don't believe you can be, for you are a traitor, a coward, and a contemptible cur. I only hope I may meet you again some time when I am off duty, and can give you the thrashing you deserve."

"All right, my young mud-lark," replied the Captain. "I'll give you a dose of medicine whenever you want it. Now clear out of here, and don't let me catch sight of you again !"

Ridge did not hear these last words, for he was already walking rapidly aft, filled with a tumult of rage and perplexity. What ought he to do? What could he do? Was ever any one so utterly helpless in a crisis of such importance? Not until he reached the extreme after part of the ship did a ray of light break upon the situation. Then he caught sight of a yacht steaming swiftly into the harbor. She might be a despatch-boat, or a destroyer, or any one of half a dozen things; but whatever she was, she could help him if she only would.

Close at hand was a jack-staff upholding an

American ensign. Acting upon the impulse of his despair, Ridge hauled down this flag, and then half-masted it, union down, thus making a signal of distress that called for prompt aid from any vessel sighting it. Then he gazed eagerly at the swiftly approaching yacht. She must have noticed his signal, for she was now headed directly for the transport, and Ridge, clinging with one hand to an awning stanchion as he stood on the rail, frantically waved his hat.

Suddenly a bellow of rage close at hand caused him to look in-board. The Captain of the transport, his face purple with passion, was rushing towards the jack-staff.

"How dare you hoist the signal of a mutiny?" he howled. "I'll show—"

"Because there is one on board," shouted Ridge, springing in front of the infuriated man, and at the same moment whipping out his revolver. "Halt where you are!" he added, fiercely. "For if you dare touch that flag before I am through with it I will blow out your traitorous brains!"

The Captain, cowed by the steadily levelled muzzle of that pistol, obeyed this order and stood still; but at the same time he yelled for any of the transport's crew who might be within hearing to tumble aft in a hurry.

In another minute they came—mates, deck-hands, engineers, stewards, and stokers—blocking the narrow gangways on either side of the deck-house. But beyond this they dared not go; for they too were confronted by that levelled pistol, and its holder's assurance that he would fire at the first man who advanced another step.

Thus the single figure with a cocked revolver and the unarmed mob that it held at bay faced each other for a full minute, during which time the purple-faced Captain raved, foamed at the mouth, and, with bitter curses, ordered his men to make a rush at the young pirate. That they did not obey was because of the unflinching steadiness of the young pirate's gaze, which they realized would detect their slightest forward movement.

All at once Ridge caught a glimpse of a man on the roof of the deck-house, just as he dodged from sight behind the life-raft  He thought he had also seen a gun in the man's hand. The next instant he sprang over the ship's rail into the sea, and as he did so a shot rang out behind him. It was not repeated when he came to the surface, for the very good reason that an armed boat from the steam-yacht was so close at hand, that ere the young trooper had cleared his eyes of salt water, its occupants were hauling him aboard.

"Sergeant Norris!" cried an amazed voice from the stern sheets. "Can it be possible?"

"Lieutenant Norris, if you please," answered our dripping hero, with what dignity he could command. "But oh, Comly! get me aboard your ship as quick as you can. It is a matter of life or death!"

"But I am ordered to investigate the mutiny on that transport." replied the bewildered Ensign.

"I am the mutiny, and in capturing me you have got the whole of it," declared Ridge. "So, as you value your future prospects, get me aboard the *Speedy*, before it shall be too late."

"All right," answered the young naval officer. "I'll risk it for your sake. So here goes."

Once on board the despatch-boat our young trooper placed the whole situation in a few words before Captain Boldwood, who no sooner comprehended it than he ordered his little ship headed up the coast with all speed.

"It will be almighty rough on the Admiral," he said to Ridge, "if Cervera comes out while he is away, after all his careful planning and weeks of weary waiting."

"What do you mean?"

"Only that Admiral Sampson has chosen to-day, of all days, to come down here for an interview with General Shafter, and we were sent ahead to make things ready for him at Siboney. He was to have followed us within half an hour; but perhaps we can turn him back in time. At any rate, we'll do our best."

So the little *Speedy* flew back over the way she had just come, displaying from her masthead as she went a string of gay bunting that read:

"The enemy's ships are escaping."

## CHAPTER XXVII

### DESTRUCTION OF THE SPANISH SHIPS

As the *Speedy* rounded the first headland those on board saw the great war-ship they were to intercept coming leisurely down the coast, not more than a mile away. The yacht fired a gun to call attention to her momentous signal, and within a few seconds an answer, showing that it was seen and understood, was displayed from the *New York*. At the same time the latter began to turn, so as to retrace her course. She had hardly begun the movement before the *Speedy* slipped up under her quarter.

"Where did you get your information?" called out Captain Chadwick through a megaphone.

"Messenger from the Commanding General," was the answer.

"All right. Keep on, and warn the fleet, if you reach them before we do."

"Ay, ay, sir!" and then the swift yacht had moved beyond range even of a megaphone.

All at once the little group of officers gathered on the *Speedy's* bridge, of course including Lieutenant Ridge Norris, knew that they were not to have the honor of warning the fleet; for a line of smoke, evidently moving seaward, appeared above the hills from the direction of Santiago Bay.

"They are coming out!" cried the *Speedy's* Captain; "and, if they have the pluck to keep on, we are about to witness one of the greatest sea-fights of the century."

If the entire American blockading fleet had been on hand the coming contest would have been too unequal to be interesting. As it was, the *Massachusetts*, *New Orleans*, and *Newark* had gone to Guantanamo after coal, while the *New York* was too far away to take any active part in the fighting. This left only the *Brooklyn*, *Oregon*, *Iowa*, *Indiana*, and *Texas* on guard, with the converted yachts *Gloucester* and *Vixen* acting as picket-boats.

The American ships lay some three miles off shore under low steam, and their crews were preparing for Sunday morning inspection. Two of the battle-ships were overhauling their forward turrets, and repairing damages received during a bombardment of the forts on the previous day. The *Brooklyn* lay farthest to the westward, and the *Indiana* at the eastern end of the line, with the *Texas*, *Iowa*, and *Oregon* between them. Inshore of these were the two yachts.

In Santiago Bay, about to rush out on these unsuspecting ships, were four of the finest cruisers in the world, possessed of greater speed than any of the Americans except the *Brooklyn*, and under a full head of steam: with them were two torpedo-boat destroyers, ranking among the most powerful and swiftest of their class.

At half-past nine o'clock of that peaceful Sunday morning, as the *Speedy* was still some five miles to the eastward of Santiago Bay, with the *New York* just completing her turn, two miles farther down the coast, a shot from the *Iowa* drew attention to her fluttering signal, "The enemy is escaping."

Almost at the same moment the same startling signal broke out from a masthead of the *Texas*, which opened the battle with the mighty roar of a twelve-inch shell. The *Brooklyn* was also flying signal 250—"The enemy is escaping"—and within three minutes from the discovery of that moving smoke behind the Morro her forward eight-inch battery was in full play against the *Maria Teresa*, first of the Spaniards to show her glistening hull around the point.

Dashing at full speed from the harbor-mouth, outlined by the smokeless flames of her forward turret and port batteries, Admiral Cervera's flag-ship was quickly headed to the westward, and for the most open point of the blockade. Behind her steamed the *Vizcaya*, *Colon*, *Oquendo*, and the torpedo-boats *Furor* and *Pluton*.

During the whole long blockade, the one standing order given by Admiral Sampson to cover an emergency like the present had been, "Should the enemy come out, close in and engage."

Now the ships that he had left on guard did close in with what speed they could command, while their sweating stokers toiled like demons in the hideous heat of the fire-rooms to produce still greater heat and more steam. As the on-rushing Spaniards cleared the harbor's mouth, every American ship was moving towards them and delivering a fire so incredibly terrific and of such deadly accuracy that its like was never known in the whole history of naval warfare.

At the outset the little *Gloucester*, commanded by Lieutenant-Commander Richard Wainwright, who had been navigating officer of the *Maine* at the time of her destruction, made a dash for her legitimate opponents, the two torpedo-boats. They in turn sought shelter behind the *Oquendo*, and for a minute it looked as though the yacht were about to attack the big cruiser. Then the *Texas* began to pay particular attention to the *Oquendo;* and, seemingly content to leave her in such good hands, the *Gloucester* again started after the destroyers. Suddenly a great shell from the *Indiana*, hurled over the yacht, struck one of them fairly amidships, and, with a roar heard high above the din of firing, the unfortunate boat plunged to the bottom, carrying with her all on board.

The *Gloucester* now directed her energies against the remaining destroyer, running well within range of the shore batteries to get at her, and within ten minutes had so riddled her with a storm of small projectiles that she lowered her colors, turned in towards the beach, struck on a reef, and in another moment was being helplessly pounded to pieces by the surf. At the same time small boats from the plucky yacht that had placed her in this sad plight were busily engaged in rescuing such of her crew as could be reached.

In the mean time both the *Teresa* and *Oquendo* had received so frightful a fire from the *Indiana*, *Iowa*, and *Texas*, that within six miles of Santiago Harbor the former, enveloped in flames, and no longer capable of defending herself, was also headed for the beach, where the gallant little *Gloucester* soon afterwards came to her assistance and rescued hundreds of her perishing crew, including brave old Admiral Cervera.

A few minutes later the *Almirante Oquendo*, with colors lowered and flames pouring from her open ports, also turned slowly inshore, and was beached within half a mile of the Spanish flag-ship. It was only forty minutes since the fight began; but in that short space four of the Spanish squadron had been destroyed, without loss of life to the Americans, and but slight damage to their ships. With the burning *Teresa* and *Oquendo* stayed the battle-ship *Indiana*, her men working in eager emulation with those of the *Gloucester* to save the lives of their recent enemies.

The next victim to succumb beneath the terrible American fire was the superb *Vizcaya*, which, pounded to death by the *Brooklyn*, *Oregon*, and *Texas*, was run on the beach at Aserraderos, seventeen miles west of Santiago Bay, a few minutes after eleven o'clock. Like her unfortunate consorts, she also was a mass of flame, and had no sooner struck than scores of her people leaped overboard to escape being roasted alive. Among these swimmers a body of Cuban troops poured a cowardly fire from the beach; but Captain Evans of the *Iowa* quickly put a stop to that, and stood by the blazing wreck so long as there was a Spaniard left to be rescued from flame or flood.

Of all Cervera's powerful squadron only a single ship was now left, the swift *Cristobal Colon*, which, by keeping behind the others, had as yet come to little harm. When the *Vizcaya* was run ashore, the *Colon* was more than four miles ahead of her leading pursuer, the *Brooklyn*. Close on the heels of the latter came the wonderful battle-ship *Oregon*, which had unexpectedly developed such extraordinary speed that, although starting next to the last of the American ships, she now very nearly led the chase. Next behind her came the *Texas*, while the superb *New York*, though still far in the rear, was overhauling all three, and had the race been long enough would eventually have exchanged broadsides with the *Colon*.

But she was not to be granted that satisfaction; for shortly after one o'clock, when the chase had lasted two hours, the *Oregon* threw a couple of great thirteen-inch shells, at a range of five miles, so close to the flying Spaniard that they deluged her with tons of water. Upon this, to the surprise of every one, and without making any sort of a fight, the finest ship of the Spanish navy lowered her flag and was headed in for the beach. After she had thus surrendered, and before the Americans could board, she was wrecked by her own crew, who opened sea-valves, smashed out dead lights, threw overboard the breech-blocks of their great guns, and in many other ways worked what destruction they could in the time allotted. As a result of this vandalism, the fine ship rolled over on her side soon after striking, and would have slipped off into deep water had not the *New York* rammed her to a better position higher up the beach.

Thus was destroyed the fine squadron that had been a menace to the Americans ever since the war began. Spain's loss was 600 human lives, 1200 prisoners, and six ships, valued at $12,000,000; while that of the Americans was one man killed and three wounded, all on the *Brooklyn*, together with a few trifling injuries to the *Brooklyn*, *Iowa*, and *Texas*.

And Ridge Norris, from the deck of the little *Speedy*, had been a spectator of the whole affair from beginning to end. Thrilled with such excitement as he had never before known, he had seen ship after ship wearing the proud colors of Spain driven helplessly to the beach by the withering blasts of Yankee gunnery, until all were destroyed. Never before had our young American been so proud of his country and his countrymen. Now his wonderful day was to be crowned with a great honor; for, no sooner was it certain that the *Colon* had surrendered, than a message from the flag-ship bade the *Speedy* return with all haste to Siboney and land the army officer whom she had brought out, that he might convey the glorious news to General Shafter and the men in the trenches before Santiago.

"That's you, old man!" cried Ensign Comly. "And I envy you your present job a heap more than I did the one you were undertaking the last time we set you ashore."

So back past the blazing wrecks of Cervera's squadron and on to Siboney dashed the despatch-boat. The transport from which Ridge had been rescued that morning still lay in the harbor, and her Captain, hailing the *Speedy*, eagerly asked for news; but none was given him, and he was treated to a contemptuous silence that caused him to grow more purple-faced than ever.

As Ridge was rowed ashore he directed Ensign Comly's attention to a large steam-yacht painted lead-color in imitation of the war-ships, but flying a Red Cross flag, that had evidently just arrived.

"She looks a little like Rollo Van Kyp's *Royal Flush*, he said; "but what is her name? G-r-a-y— Gray man? Gray mare? Oh no, *Gray Nun*. Queer name for a yacht, isn't it?"

"Yes; and those nurses on her deck don't look a bit like nuns," replied Ensign Comly. "Believe I'll make a call if we lie here this evening, for I understand that some of the nicest girls in the country have enlisted under the Red Cross since you chaps were sent to Santiago."

"Wish I could join you," sighed Ridge; "only I haven't spoken to a girl in so long that I shouldn't know what to say."

## CHAPTER XXVIII

### LAST SHOT OF THE CAMPAIGN

THE American army occupying the muddy trenches before Santiago had been rendered very unhappy that morning by a rumor that Cervera's ships had made a dash from the harbor, evaded the blockade, and escaped almost unharmed. How this rumor started no one knew, but it spread like wildfire, and was generally believed. There was ample opportunity for discussing it, since all firing had ceased, while under a flag of truce an envoy from General Shafter demanded the surrender of Santiago. So the men in the trenches were free to stand erect and stretch themselves, to wander about, leaving their rifles in position between the sandbags, and even to make little fires, over which to boil cups of coffee, all without drawing the fire of a single Spanish sharp-shooter. It was a very novel sensation, and they enjoyed it. At the same time they were not happy, for Cervera's ships had escaped. What could the Yankee sailors have been about to let such a thing happen? What a disgrace it was, and how the whole world would jeer! Even Santiago seemed hardly worth capturing now.

All at once a sound of shouting was borne faintly to their ears from the distant rear. What had happened? Had they been outflanked by the Spaniards and attacked from that direction? No, for a band was playing on El Poso Hill, and the sound of shouting was advancing, like a roar of the sea. No one looked towards Santiago now, but all eyes, turned to the rear, were fixed on the point where the Sevilla road left the timber. At this place they gazed in eager but silent anticipation. Suddenly a horseman emerged from it and dashed at full speed across the valley, waving his hat and yelling as he came.

Up the slope of San Juan Hill he charged and through the terraced camps, that broke into a jubilant roar as he reached them. But he did not pause until he had gained the very trenches, where among the wondering Rough Riders he slipped wearily from his foam-flecked horse, shouting huskily but exultantly as he did so:

"Sampson has destroyed the Spanish fleet! Not a ship escaped! I know, for I saw the whole fight!"

"Hurrah!" "Hooray!" "Whoop-ee!" "Wow, wow, wow!" howled the Riders, as in their wild jubilation they danced, hugged each other, and flung things in the air. Then they raised Ridge high on their shoulders and bore him as proudly aloft as though he alone had achieved the wonderful victory of which he brought the news. Indeed, they seemed to believe that but for his presence with the American ships things might perhaps have gone differently, and Rollo Van Kyp only voiced the general sentiment when he said:

"Lucky thing for Sampson that he had at least one 'Terror' along to see that the scrap was conducted according to rules. How I wish, though, that the *Nun* had got here in time to take part in that fight, for she can outfoot the old *Corsair—Gloucester*, I mean—almost two to one. If she had only been on hand I believe she would have captured one of these little fellows alive, before he had a chance to make the beach."

"The who?" asked Ridge, in perplexity, for the latter part of this remark had been addressed to him alone.

"The *Nun*. *Gray Nun* is her whole name. My yacht—used to be the *Royal Flush*, you know. I offered her to the government as a gift, to be converted into a war-ship. But they wouldn't accept her. So I changed her name, and turned her over to the Red Cross people, to use as long as they had need of her. Don't know, though, as they took me up, for we left about that time, and I haven't heard since."

"But they did!" exclaimed Ridge. "And she reached Siboney to-day, for I saw her there not more than two hours ago, flying a Red Cross flag, and crowded with nurses."

"Good enough!" cried Rollo. "That is almost as fine news as the other. The old *Flush* must feel funny, though, all cluttered up with nurses, for that isn't exactly the kind of a crowd she has been used to. Same time, if my steward carried out the orders I wired him, she must be loaded to the muzzle with good things to eat and drink, for I told him to fill her up with the best to be had in New York City. So if any of the fellows are hankering for a change of grub, all they've got to do is to catch a fever or a Mauser bullet, and apply for a berth on the *Nun*. For my own part I prefer hardtack, bacon, and good health; but then tastes differ, you know."

"It was a splendid thing to do!" exclaimed Ridge; "and I don't believe there is another in the command would have thought of it. The boys will be prouder than ever of the old regiment to know that it contains a fellow not only able but willing to do such a thing."

"Oh, pshaw!" replied Rollo, flushing. "There isn't one but would do as much and more, only some of them don't happen to have yachts lying idle. And you mustn't tell them, old man. I wouldn't for anything have it get out that the *Nun* is my boat. That's the reason I changed her name. Some of them might think I was putting on airs, you know, if it should get out that I kept my yacht here at Siboney."

"But you'll get leave to run down and see her, won't you?"

"Not much, I won't. The dear old skipper would be sure to give me away, though his orders are not to mention my name in connection with her."

So the bountiful supply of delicacies and comforts of every kind provided by Rollo Van Kyp were distributed among the sick and wounded in the Siboney hospitals, and many a fever-stricken patient owed his life to the devoted care of the "gray nuns," as the nurses brought by the yacht were generally called; but only Ridge Norris knew whose was the generous forethought that had provided all these things.

In the mean time the truce, first declared on that memorable Sunday, was extended from day to day, for one reason or another, for a week. General Linares had been wounded early in the fighting, General Vara del Rey had been killed at Caney, and the command of Santiago had finally devolved upon General Toral. To him, then, was sent the summons to surrender. This he refused to do, but begged for time in which to remove women, children, and other non-combatants from the city before it should be bombarded. This was allowed, and nearly 20,000 of these helpless ones, frightened, bewildered, and half famished, were driven from Santiago to seek such refuge as the surrounding country might afford. War-wrecked and devastated as it was, its resources in the way of food and shelter were so slender that hundreds of them died from exposure, starvation, or disease, and but for the generosity of the Americans, who fed them to the full extent of their ability, thousands more must have perished.

And others came out from the beleaguered city; for an exchange of prisoners had been effected, and just before sunset on the third day of the truce three horsemen rode towards the American lines along the palm-shaded highway leading from Santiago. Two of them were Spanish officers, but one wore the white duck uniform of the American navy, and behind him clattered an ambulance in which were seven of the proudest, happiest sailormen ever turned loose from an enemy's prison. They were Hobson and his men, the heroes of the *Merrimac*, free at last to return to their own people. And never did heroes receive a more royal welcome than that accorded this handful of blue-jackets by their comrades of the army. From the outermost trenches all the way to Siboney, where a launch awaited them, their progress was an ovation of wildest enthusiasm. Every soldier of the thousands whom they encountered first saluted and then cheered until he was hoarse, while one regimental band after another crashed forth its most inspiring music in their honor. Out on the star-lit sea lay the great flag-ship from which these men had departed on their desperate mission more than a month before, and when, late that evening, they again reached it, they were once more safe at home with their work well done, and their fame established forever.

For a week the truce continued, and while the Spaniards strengthened their defences, the Americans lengthened their lines, built roads over which to bring up their artillery, provided their camps with bomb-proof shelters, and received reinforcements. Knowing all this, General Toral still refused to surrender, and during the afternoon of Sunday, July 10th, the white flags were taken down and a bombardment of the city was begun. For two hours, or until the coming of darkness, a heavy cannonade with brisk rifle-fire was kept up by both sides, but with little damage to either. With sunrise of the following morning it was resumed.

"I wonder what it is all for?" asked Rollo Van Kyp, as he crouched in the hot trench, industriously firing his carbine at the flashes from the Spanish rifle-pits. "We don't seem to hit them, and they certainly don't hit us. Now if Teddy would only order a charge, it would be something sensible. But this play-fighting is disgusting!"

Just then a Spanish shell burst close above the heads of this particular group of Rough Riders, and a fragment from it cut the staff of the troop guidon, planted in the soft earth, so that the silken flag fell outward. In an instant Rollo had leaped over the protecting embankment, picked up the fallen flag, and, amid yells of approbation from his comrades, restored it to its former position. Then, half-turning and swinging his hat defiantly above his head, the daring young trooper sprang back to his place of safety. As he did so, something seemed to go wrong, and instead of landing on his feet he pitched awkwardly, and then lay motionless in the bottom of the trench.

At the same moment trumpet and bugle along the whole line sounded the order "cease firing," and once more the white flags of truce fluttered in the sunlight. Santiago was again summoned to surrender; and this time the summons was so seriously considered that, two days later, it was obeyed. Although no one knew it at the time, the last shot of the campaign had been fired and the war was virtually ended.

But the last shot had stricken down brave, generous, light-hearted Rollo Van Kyp just as he had covered himself with glory and was within a hair's-breadth of safety; for, as Lieutenant Norris knelt anxiously beside his friend, the gallant young trooper lay as though dead, with blood streaming over his face.

## CHAPTER XXIX

### TWO INVALID HEROES

ROLLO VAN KYP, carefully lifted from the bloody trench in which he had fought and suffered so cheerfully, was borne to the rear, and the assistant surgeon of his regiment accompanied him to the hospital at Siboney. Ridge Norris wanted to do this, but his duties would not permit of his absence, for officers were becoming scarce, and as yet no one knew but that the fighting might be resumed at any moment. So he watched the departure of the ambulance with a heavy heart, and the whole troop shared his sorrow at the loss of their well-loved comrade.

The next day the assistant surgeon returned and reported Rollo's wound apparently so serious that there was little hope for him. "There was just one chance," he added, in answer to Lieutenant Norris's anxious inquiry for details, "and, by good luck, I secured it for him at the last moment. He would surely have died in Siboney, but if he can get home and into a Northern hospital he may pull through. By the greatest good fortune a Red Cross ship was about to start for the States with a number of the worst cases; and, just as she was sailing, I managed to get Van Kyp aboard. She was so crowded that they weren't going to take him, until her skipper— as big-hearted a Yankee sailorman as ever trod a deck—said he would give up his own cabin rather than have a Rough Rider left behind to die."

"What was his name?" asked Ridge.

"Haven't an idea."

"Do you know the name of the ship?"

"Yes, of course. She is the *Gray Nun*, a converted yacht."

"Rollo Van Kyp's own boat!" cried Ridge.

"You don't mean it?"

"I do." And then Ridge told all that he knew of his friend's splendid contribution to the service that was doing more than the government itself towards alleviating the sufferings of the American troops before Santiago. When he finished, he said, "Of course the skipper recognized Van Kyp?"

"No, he didn't," replied the other—"at least, not then, for the poor chap's face was covered to protect it from the sun, and I didn't mention his name until after he had been taken aboard, when I gave it to the surgeon in charge. At first I only described him as a Rough Rider wounded in recovering his troop flag, and the skipper said that was all he wanted to know about him."

Besides his news of Rollo, the surgeon had brought from Siboney a number· of letters recently arrived there for the Rough Riders, and one of these was handed to Ridge. Opening it curiously, for he did not recognize the handwriting of its address, the latter read as follows:

"DEAR MR. NORRIS,—I have just been made very happy by learning from a friend of yours, a Mr. Comly, who is in the navy, that you are not only alive and well, but still with your regiment, and have done all sorts of splendid things. This is news that will cause great rejoicing among all your friends, including your own family, who have been very anxious and unhappy concerning you. Major Dodley reported in New Orleans that you had been placed under arrest for desertion—of course no one who knew you believed that for a moment—but had escaped and run away. Your father was so furious that he gave the Major a horsewhipping in front of the St. Charles, and made him take back every word. Then he telegraphed and wrote to Tampa; but half of your regiment had left, and those who remained behind could tell nothing except that you had disappeared in a very mysterious manner. You may imagine the distress of your father.

"I had returned to my own home, but Dulce wrote me all about it, and I received her letter when on the point of starting for New York to offer my services as a Red Cross nurse, for I didn't feel that I could let the war go on a day longer without having some share in it. I was accepted, and immediately assigned to duty aboard the society's ship *Gray Nun*, to which I am still attached. That is how I happen to be here, and I am so glad I came, for I don't believe even you can imagine how much we were needed. I have also discovered you, and shall write to Dulce at once. Hoping that we may meet before long, I remain,
"Very sincerely your friend,
"SPENCE CUTHBERT.
"On board *Gray Nun*, off Siboney, *July* 8, 1898."

"Whew!" whistled Ridge, softly, as he finished reading this letter. "If that isn't a budget of news! Spence Cuthbert here in Cuba nursing wounded soldiers! But it is just like the dear girl to do such a thing. If I had only known of it sooner, though, I might have found a chance to run down to Siboney and see her. Now it is too late, for the *Nun* has gone again. She will discover Rollo, though, and take care of him. Lucky fellow! Wish I was in his place! And Comly, too! He must have made that call and scraped an acquaintance. What cheek those navy chaps have, anyway! So Dodley reports me as a deserter, does he? And the dear old dad horsewhipped him. Oh, if I had only been there! It is a shame that I haven't managed to write home, and I'll do so this very minute."

In pursuance of this resolve, Ridge did write a long letter to his mother, in which he told of his great disappointment at not seeing Spence Cuthbert before she left Cuba, and sent it to Siboney to be forwarded at the first opportunity.

After that, other exciting events in connection with his duty occupied our young Lieutenant's attention; for at a meeting of Generals Shafter and Toral, under a great tree midway between the American and Spanish lines, the latter finally agreed to surrender the entire province of Santiago, with all the troops within its limits. On this occasion each General was accompanied by members of his staff, and to Ridge again fell the honor of acting as official interpreter. Thus for days he

RIDGE ESCORTS A CUBAN FAMILY INTO SANTIAGO

was kept so continually busy that he hardly found time for sleep. Then, on Sunday, the 17th of July, one week after the firing of the last shot, and two weeks after the destruction of Cervera's ships, at precisely noon, the red and yellow banner of Spain was lowered forever from over Santiago's municipal palace, and the glorious stars and stripes proudly flung to the breeze in its place. The impressive ceremony was witnessed by the Ninth Regiment of United States Infantry, two mounted troops of the Second Regular Cavalry, and by the brilliant staff who surrounded General Shafter. Besides these, Spanish officers and citizens of Santiago crowded every window, doorway, and portico of the cathedral, the San Carlos Club, the Venus restaurant, and other buildings facing the Plaza de Armas, and watched the proceedings in silence.

As the starry flag of the United States ran slowly to the top of the tall staff the Ninth Regiment band crashed forth the inspiring strains of "The Star-spangled Banner," and every American present, excepting, of course, the troops on duty, bared his head. At the same moment the thunder of distant artillery firing a national salute of twenty-one guns and exultant cheering from the trenches a mile beyond the city told that the glorious news had reached the waiting army.

At the conclusion of the ceremony, General Leonard Wood, formerly Colonel of the Rough Riders, was installed as Military Governor of the conquered city, and one of the first to congratulate him upon this new honor was the young Lieutenant of his old command, who had been permitted to do so much towards bringing the Santiago campaign to its happy conclusion. For Ridge Norris, in appreciation of his recent services, had been one of the very few guests invited to witness the change of flags.

Shortly after it was all over, as Ridge was slowly making his way back to camp, no longer upheld by excitement and utterly weary from his recent labors, he encountered a forlorn little group of natives, who aroused his instant sympathy. A young woman, gaunt and hollow-cheeked, with three children, trying to make her way back to the city, had sunk exhausted by the road-side. One of the children was a babe held tightly pressed to her bosom. Of the others, one was a small boy, who stood manfully by his mother's side; while a little girl, burning with fever, lay tossing and moaning on the ground.

As Ridge reached this group the woman cried, imploringly, "Help, Señor Americano! For love of the good God help me reach the city before my little ones perish!"

Ridge could understand and could talk to her in her own tongue. So in a few minutes he had learned her pitiful story. It was that of many another—a tale of starvation, sickness, death of her husband, and of homeless wandering for days. Now her one desire and hope was to return to her home in Santiago. Even before she had concluded her sad narration our young trooper had picked up the fever-stricken child, and, with the others following him, was retracing his steps towards the city. He did not leave them until they were safe in the wretched hovel they called home, and he had procured for them a supply of food. Then, followed by fervent blessings, he again started for the American lines.

That evening he could not eat the coarse camp fare of his mess, and the next morning found him raving in the delirium of fever. When, a little later, the Rough Riders were removed to a more healthful camp-ground, a few miles back in the hills, Lieutenant Norris, with several other fever-stricken members of the command, was taken to one of the Spanish hospitals in Santiago, where, three days later, Spence Cuthbert found him.

## CHAPTER XXX

### ROLLO MAKES PROPOSITIONS

THE month of August was drawing to its close when an expectant throng of people gathered about the wharf of the great military camp recently established for the home-returning American army at Montauk Point, on the extreme eastern end of Long Island. Most of the throng were soldiers, but among them was a little group of civilians accompanied by a young trooper wearing a brand-new uniform, but looking very pale and weak, as though recovering from a severe illness. He was Rollo Van Kyp, only just out from the New York hospital to which he had been taken more than a month before. With him, and anticipating his every need, were Mr. and Mrs. Norris and Dulce. Their Long Island summer home had not been sold, and now there was no need that it should be, since Mr. Norris's affairs had taken a decided turn for the better. As soon, therefore, as they learned that the army was to be sent to Montauk, they went to this cottage and fitted it up as a convalescent hospital, for any of their boy's wounded comrades to whom he might desire to show particular attention. Thus

Dulce, though not enrolled in the Red Cross service, wore a nurse's costume, and Rollo Van Kyp, who had insisted on coming down to welcome his home-returning comrades, was one of her patients. Now they were looking for Ridge, of whose illness they had not yet learned.

Those Rough Riders left behind at Tampa had already been transferred to Montauk, together with all the horses of the regiment, and these hearty young troopers formed the greater part of the throng now assembled to greet the heroes of Las Guasimas, of San Juan, and of the Santiago trenches, for Colonel Roosevelt and his men were coming home, and the *Miami*, on which they were embarked, was nearing the wharf. Her decks were crowded with men, worn and weary, clad in battle-stained uniforms, and filled with a great joy at once more breathing the air of their native land. Already was Rollo recognizing familiar faces, and eagerly pointing them out.

"But where is my boy?" cried Mrs. Norris. "I cannot see him."

The others did not answer, for they too were greatly disappointed at not discovering the face they most longed to see.

At length the slow-moving ship was made fast, its gang-plank was run out, and the eager troopers began to swarm ashore. Some were so weak that comrades were obliged to support their feeble steps; but all were radiant with the joy of home-coming. Cheer after cheer greeted each troop, as with silken guidons fluttering above them they marched from the ship, and finally a perfect roar of welcome announced the appearance of their Colonel.

"There's Teddy!" cried Rollo, with a feeble attempt at waving his hat. "Oh, how good it is to see him again!"

"But my boy! Where is my boy?" cried the distracted mother, crowding her way to the very front rank of spectators. As she did so, Colonel Roosevelt passed close to her, and she clutched his arm.

"Oh, sir, my boy! Where is my boy? Do not tell me he is dead!"

"It is Mrs. Norris, Colonel," explained Rollo Van Kyp, pressing forward, "and she is disappointed at not seeing the Lieutenant."

"Thank God, my dear fellow, that you are alive!" exclaimed the Colonel, grasping Van Kyp's hand. Then, in a lower tone, he added, "We had to leave poor Norris behind. He was too ill to be brought on a transport, but he may come at any time on a hospital-ship. Here is a note for his family from one of the hospital nurses. My dear madam," he added, turning to Mrs. Norris, "your son is alive, but detained for a time at Santiago. If you will excuse me now, I will see you again very shortly, and tell you of all the fine things he has done."

With this the embarrassed Colonel passed on, thankful at having thus concluded one of the interviews with anxious parents that he so dreaded.

For a moment Mrs. Norris stared after him in speechless agony; for the mother's keen ear had overheard his low-spoken words to Rollo Van Kyp, and she knew that her boy had been left in Cuba too ill to be moved. Then she uttered a moan, and fainted in her husband's arms.

A little later, when the saddened group had been driven back to the cottage that had been so happily prepared for the reception of their soldier, they read Spence Cuthbert's note, hastily written as the Rough Riders were embarking at Santiago. It told of the terrible suffering that had impelled her to remain behind when the *Gray Nun* went north, of her disappointment at not hearing anything from Ridge, and how she had at last discovered him in the Santiago hospital, to which she had been transferred immediately after the surrender.

"I did not dare write sooner," she continued, "for we had no hope that he could live; but now he is again conscious, and has recognized me. The doctors talk of sending him north as soon as he can be moved; but, remembering the horrors of the *Seneca* and the *Concho*, I dread the voyage for him even more than I do the pestilent air of this awful hospital. In fact, I am in despair, and know not what is best to be done."

"I know!" exclaimed Rollo Van Kyp, as Dulce, with tear-filled eyes, finished reading this pitiful note. "He must be brought back on the *Nun*. Mr. Norris, she leaves New York to-morrow with a fresh lot of nurses for Santiago, and if you will only take the run down on her you can bring the dear old chap back in comfort."

Mr. Norris hesitated a moment. "Do you realize," he asked, "that if your yacht brings back a single yellow-fever patient it may never be safe to use her again?"

"My dear sir!" cried Rollo, "if she were all that I had in the world she would still be at the service of my dearest friend."

So Mr. Norris thankfully accepted the young millionaire's offer, and sailed the very next day for Santiago.

A week later a Red Cross nurse, worn and wearied almost to the point of exhaustion by her days and nights of caring for sick and dying soldiers, sat in a Santiago hospital beside one of her patients, gently fanning him. His eyes were closed, and she hoped that he slept. As she watched him her own eyes slowly filled with tears; for she did not believe he would ever gain sufficient strength to bear removal from that house of sorrow. The air of the ward was hot, damp, and lifeless. Sickening odors rising from the streets of the filthy city drifted in through its open windows. The whole atmosphere of the place was depressing, and suggestive of suffering that could only end with death.

"Poor Ridge!" she murmured bitterly to herself. "After all your splended work, it is cruel to leave you here to die, deserted and forgotten!"

Just then the patient opened wide his eyes, and an expression of eager anticipation flitted across his white face. "Dad is coming," he whispered. "I hear his footstep. Oh, Spence, he is here, and will take us home!"

The nurse listened, but heard only the moans of other sufferers, and thinking that this one had dreamed of his father's coming, tried to soothe him with hopeful promises. Then, all at once, she uttered a little cry of joy, for at the far end of the long white ward she saw one of the house surgeons escorting a familiar figure. In another minute Mr. Norris, seeming to bring with him a breath of bracing northern air, stood beside his son's cot.

"I thank God and you, Spence Cuthbert, that my boy is still alive!" he cried. "And now, how soon can we take him north? I have Van Kyp's yacht waiting out here in the harbor, and we can start at a moment's notice."

"I believe I could go this very minute, dad," said Ridge, his voice already strengthened with hope and happiness. "But, father," he added, anxiously, "we must take Spence with us; for she has promised to stay with me as long as I need her, and I know I couldn't travel without her."

"Of course we will take her, son, and keep her, too, just as long as we can."

For three days longer Ridge lay on that cot, gaining strength with each moment of renewed hope and eager anticipation. During this time Mr. Norris occupied the intervals of rest from watching beside his son with visiting the battle-fields near the city over which the young trooper had so bravely fought. On these expeditions he was accompanied and guided by a Cuban named del Concha, recommended by General Wood, to whom he had rendered valuable service by the giving of intelligent and honestly patriotic advice. When del Concha discovered that the American señor whom he was asked to guide was father to his friend, the brave *teniente* Norris, he was overjoyed to be of assistance to him, and completely won the elder gentleman's heart by praise of his son and stories of the latter's exploits while executing his dangerous mission among the Spaniards of Cuba. Del Concha also told of himself; and, among other things, that, on the very day he had learned of Santiago's surrender, he had married his sweetheart, the brave girl who had assisted Ridge to escape from the Holguin prison, and who was now very nearly recovered from her wound.

At length the joyous day came when Ridge could be moved, and he was carefully borne in a litter, by four of the stalwart negro troopers, in whose company he had charged up San Juan Heights, through the streets of Santiago to the waiting yacht. Besides the young trooper and his proud father, the *Nun* carried northward a score more of convalescent soldiers, to whom Spence Cuthbert, and a group of her companion nurses, also returning home from their glorious service, gave devoted care.

On the day that Montauk was to be reached, Ridge was strong enough to be carried on deck, where, from a pillowed steamer-chair, he gazed happily at the loved features of the nearing coast.

He was the very first to spy his mother, who again waited in trembling eagerness on the wharf, this time not to be disappointed.

"And there are Rollo," he said, to the girl who stood beside him, "and Dulce, and the Colonel. And oh, Spence, to think that but for you I should certainly never have seen them again!"

For many days after the home-coming of our young trooper the Norris cottage was strictly quarantined against a possible outbreak of yellow-fever; but, as Rollo Van Kyp said:

"Who cares? I'm sure I don't; for all of the world I want to see just now is held within these walls."

The very first time Ridge was allowed to go out, he was driven to the Rough-Rider camp to be mustered from service with his regiment. On this occasion he wore a lieutenant's uniform, at which his mother, seated beside him in the carriage, gazed with such undisguised pride that he laughingly accused her of being more susceptible to the influence of brass buttons than any girl of his acquaintance.

Only once after this did our young lieutenant wear his uniform, and that was when, two months later, he was married in a little Kentucky church to Spence Cuthbert, who, at his earnest request, wore as her wedding-dress the costume of a Red Cross nurse.

Dulce was, of course, maid of honor, while Rollo Van Kyp was best man. When the simple ceremony was over, and they were all gathered to wish the radiant couple God-speed on their wedding journey, Rollo unfolded the great news he had received that morning.

"Teddy has been nominated for Governor of New York!" he cried. "And I am to stump the State with him. When he is elected he is going to make me a Colonel on his staff, so that Dulce won't have to marry a mere private after all."

And Dulce, blushing furiously, replied, "I would rather marry a private soldier who had charged up San Juan Hill than any staff-officer in the world."

"How about taking both?" asked Rollo.

THE END

BOSTON PUBLIC LIBRARY

3 9999 05676 959 7

www.ingramcontent.com/pod-product-compliance
Lightning Source LLC
Chambersburg PA
CBHW032122230426
43672CB00009B/1826